# Bahamas

# Primary Social Studies

**Grade 6**

Lisa Greenstein
Karen Morrison

## Acknowledgements

Every effort has been made to trace all copyright holders, but if any have been inadvertently overlooked, the Publishers will be pleased to make the necessary arrangements at the first opportunity.

Although every effort has been made to ensure that website addresses are correct at time of going to press, Hodder Education cannot be held responsible for the content of any website mentioned in this book. It is sometimes possible to find a relocated web page by typing in the address of the home page for a website in the URL window of your browser.

Hachette UK's policy is to use papers that are natural, renewable and recyclable products and made from wood grown in well-managed forests and other controlled sources. The logging and manufacturing processes are expected to conform to the environmental regulations of the country of origin.

Orders: please contact Hachette UK Distribution, Hely Hutchinson Centre, Milton Road, Didcot, Oxfordshire, OX11 7HH. Telephone: +44 (0)1235 827827. Email education@hachette.co.uk Lines are open from 9 a.m. to 5 p.m., Monday to Friday. You can also order through our website: www.hoddereducation.com

ISBN: 9781398390102

© Lisa Greenstein and Karen Morrison 2023

First published in 2023 by

Hodder Education,
An Hachette UK Company
Carmelite House
50 Victoria Embankment
London EC4Y 0DZ

www.hoddereducation.com

Impression number 10 9 8 7 6 5 4 3 2 1

Year 2026 2025 2024 2023



Cover photo © Mustafa AlSorougi – stock.adobe.com

Illustrations by Rassie Erasmus, Vian Oelofsen, Stéphan Theron

Typeset in 12 on 16pt FS Albert

Printed in Spain

A catalogue record for this title is available from the British Library.

### Text acknowledgements

**p. 80** Source: https://www.ramblebahamas.org/items/show/12; © Jessica Dawson & Tracey Thompson, «The Contract», Ramble Bahamas, accessed July 2023 ,4, https://www.ramblebahamas.org/items/show/12. https://creativecommons.org/licenses/by/4.0/; **p. 85** © Saunders, Gail, ‹The 1958 General Strike and Its Aftermath›, Race and Class in the Colonial Bahamas, 1960-1880 (Gainesville, FL, 2016; online edn, Florida Scholarship Online, 19 Jan. 2017), https://doi.org/10.5744/florida/9780813062549.003.0009, accessed 4 July 2023; **p. 85** © https://api.parliament.uk/historic-hansard/commons/1958/jan/30/general-strike. https://www.parliament.uk/site-information/copyright-parliament/open-parliament-licence/.

### Photo acknowledgements

**p. 4** *br*, **p. 12** *cc, cr* © Hachette; **p. 6** *cl* © mozZz/stock.adobe.com; **p. 6** *bl*, **p. 45** *cr* © YuI/stock.adobe.com; **p. 7** *cr* © Tarik GOK/stock.adobe.com; **p. 7** *cr* © Tarik GOK/stock.adobe.com; **p. 7** *cr* © aomvector/stock.adobe.com; **p. 7** *cr* © Tarik GOK/stock.adobe.com; **p. 7** *br* © grgroup/stock.adobe.com; **p. 9** *tr* © Momcilica/Shutterstock.com; **p. 9** *cr*, **p. 77** *cc* © Jaume Ollé/https://creativecommons.org/licenses/by-sa/3.0/; **p. 16** *cl* © Universal Images Group North America LLC/Alamy Stock Photo; **p. 19** *tc* © Peter Hermes Furian/stock.adobe.com; **p. 19** *bc* © bogdanserban/stock.adobe.com; **p. 20** *tl* © Curioso.Photography/stock.adobe.com; **p. 20** *tr* © ladsv/stock.adobe.com; **p. 20** *cl* © Alex254/Wirestock Creators/stock.adobe.com; **p. 20** *cr* © Greg Brave/stock.adobe.com; **p. 20** *bl* © Kavalenkava/stock.adobe.com; **p. 20** *br* © Robert/stock.adobe.com; **p. 22** *br* © Designpics/stock.adobe.com; **p. 23** *cl* © Dimitrios Karamitros/Shutterstock.com; **p. 24** *br* © Fly_and_Dive/stock.adobe.com; **p. 26** *br* © blueringmedia/stock.adobe.com; **p. 38** *tl* © Zoran Karapancev/Shutterstock.com; **p. 38** *tl* © 2023-2018 Judiciary The Bahamas. Designed and Developed by Starboard Softworks, Ltd.; **p. 40** © 2023-2018 Judiciary The Bahamas. Designed and Developed by Starboar d Softworks, Ltd.; **p. 45** *tc* © Iuliia/stock.adobe.com; **p. 45** *tr* © liana2012/stock.adobe.com; **p. 45** *cc* © 1jaimages/stock.adobe.com; **p. 47** *cl* © royalbahamaspolice.org/https://creativecommons.org/licenses/by-sa/4.0/deed.en; **p. 47** *cc* © bahamas.gov.bs/https://creativecommons.org/licenses/by-sa/4.0/deed.en; **p. 47** *cr* © bahamas.gov.bs; **p. 50** *tl* © offsuperphoto/stock.adobe.com; **p. 50** *cl* © amorn/stock.adobe.com; **p. 50** *cl* © Maksym Kapliuk/stock.adobe.com; **p. 50** *bl* © sezerozger/stock.adobe.com; **p. 51** *tr* © majeczka/stock.adobe.com; **p. 51** *cr* © jzehnder/stock.adobe.com; **p. 51** *cr* © Wollwerth Imagery/stock.adobe.com; **p. 51** *br* © allexxandarx/stock.adobe.com; **p. 52** *bl* © Ministry of the Environment and Natural Resources; **p. 53** *cc* © United Nations; **p. 55** *cr* © mehaniq41/stock.adobe.com; **p. 57** *cr* © moofushi/stock.adobe.com; **p. 57** *cr* © Tayjowkup/stock.adobe.com; **p. 59** *cl* © Jane Kelly/stock.adobe.com; **p. 64** *cl* © kehinde/stock.adobe.com; **p. 64** *cc* © Nordroden/stock.adobe.com; **p. 64** *cr* © NVB Stocker/stock.adobe.com; **p. 64** *bl* © melnikofd/stock.adobe.com; **p. 64** *bc* © Juozas55/stock.adobe.com; **p. 64** *br* © Mavo Images/Shutterstock.com; **p. 66** *cr* © White bear studio/stock.adobe.com; **p. 67** *cl* © corvalola/stock.adobe.com; **p. 67** *cc* © Cobalt/stock.adobe.com; **p. 67** *cc* © angelmaxmixam/stock.adobe.com; **p. 67** *cr* © Viacheslav/stock.adobe.com; **p. 67** *bl* © aigarsr/stock.adobe.com; **p. 67** *bc* © Abdallavector/Shutterstock.com; **p. 67** *bc* © Icons-Studio/stock.adobe.com; **p. 67** *bc* © FR Design/stock.adobe.com; **p. 67** *br* © FR Design/stock.adobe.com; **p. 68** *cl* © Yolanda Oltra/Alamy Stock Photo; **p. 69** *cr* © WavebreakMediaMicro/stock.adobe.com; **p. 71** *cl, cc*, **p. 99** *br* © Mike van der Wolk 27832686000+ mike@springhigh.co.za; **p. 76** *br* © Jadesada/Shutterstock.com; **p. 78** *tc* © jerzy/stock.adobe.com; **p. 78** *tr* © James Quine/Alamy Stock Photo; **p. 79** *cr* © INTERFOTO/Alamy Stock Photo; **p. 81** *cr* © Syda Productions/stock.adobe.com; **p. 83** *cr* © Bettmann/Contributor/Getty Images; **p. 87** *cr* © Sergey Goryachev/Shutterstock.com; **p. 88** *cr* © pepifoto/Getty Images; **p. 89** *bc* © Navin/stock.adobe.com; **p. 94** *cl* © Popperfoto/Contributor/Getty Images; **p. 94** *cr* © Reuters/Alamy Stock Photo; **p. 94** *cc* © John Gichigi/Getty Images; **p. 95** *tl* ©dpa picture alliance/Alamy Stock Photo; **p. 95** *tr* © Naoki Morita/AFLO SPORT/Alamy Live News; **p. 96** *cr* ©Juliet Highet/ArkReligion.com/Alamy Stock Photo; **p. 98** *cl* © Michael DeFreitas Caribbean/Alamy Stock Photo; **p. 98** *cc* © JAFER/stock.adobe.com; **p. 98** *cr* © Fanfo/stock.adobe.com; **p. 98** *bl* © Rarity Asset Club/stock.adobe.com; **p. 98** *bc* © SunnyS/stock.adobe.com; **p. 98** *br* © SuperStock/Alamy Stock Photo; **p. 100** *tr* © Montez Kerr/Alamy Stock Photo; **p. 102** *cc* © melita/stock.adobe.com; **p. 103** *cr* © livcool/Shutterstock.com; **p. 103** *cl* © Taras Vyshnya/stock.adobe.com; **p. 103** *br* © rashmisingh/stock.adobe.com; **p. 104** *tr* © Fotoluminate LLC/stock.adobe.com; **p. 104** *cl* © Andrew Mayovskyy/stock.adobe.com; **p. 104** *br* © exclusive-design/stock.adobe.com; **p. 105** *tl* © Anna Om/stock.adobe.comk; **p. 105** *cr* © Flavia Novais/stock.adobe.com; **p. 105** *br* © StanislavBeloglazov/Shutterstock.com.

*t* = top, *b* = bottom, *l* = left, *r* = right, *c* = centre

# Contents

# Introduction

Welcome to *Bahamas Primary Social Studies Grade 6*.

The book is divided into three **themes**:
- **Theme 1**   Our Bahamian identity, our pride
- **Theme 2**   Cooperation and industry
- **Theme 3**   Our Bahamian heritage

You will work through one theme during each school term. The themes follow the curriculum guidelines set out by the Ministry of Education of The Bahamas.

The **Contents** page before this Introduction helps you to locate the themes and units in this book.

Each theme is divided into various units. Some units are longer than others. Shorter units may take a lesson or two to complete; longer units may take a week or two.

Your teacher will help to guide you through each unit. This is what you will find in each unit:

**Unit name**

**Unit number**

**Objectives** list the main content of the unit

**Headings** help guide you through the text with sub-headings also sometimes used for sub-topics within the main heading

**Word power** lists vocabulary words. You can find definitions for these words in the **Glossary** at the back of the book

**Pictures**

**Labels** sometimes appear around pictures to help you understand more about them.

**Captions** tell you more about the pictures

**Text** gives you information you can use to complete the activities

**Page number**

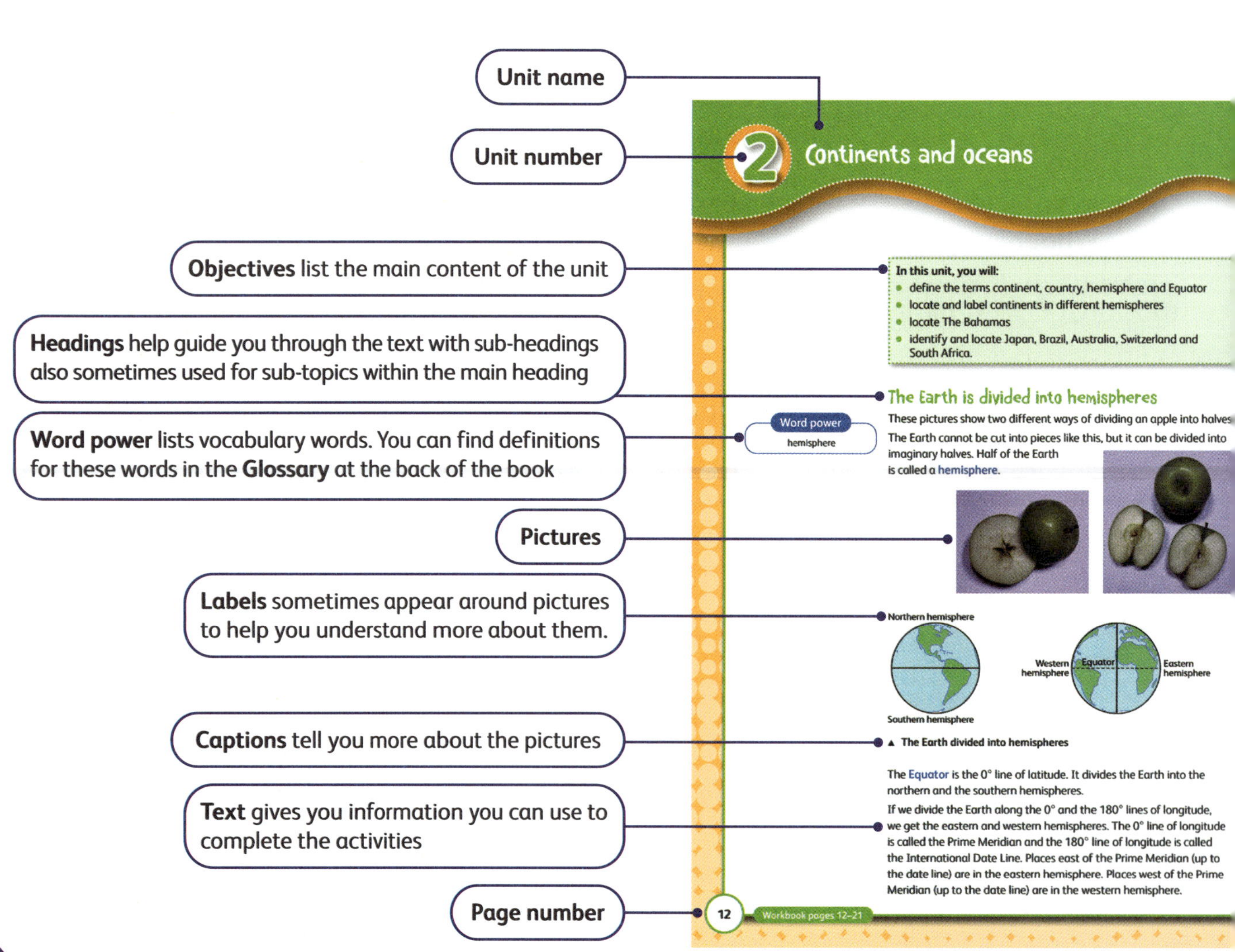

Other features you may notice in a unit are the following:

- **Did you know?** boxes give extra bits of interesting information.
- **Tips** boxes give you extra guidance for your learning.
- **Case study** boxes provide examples of how the ideas you are learning about apply to real-life situations.
- **Reflection** boxes help you to think back over what you have learnt in each unit.









At the end of each theme, a **What have you learnt?** section helps you to revise the units that were covered in that theme.

Finally, at the end of the book you will find a **Glossary**, with a list of all the **Word power** words and their definitions.

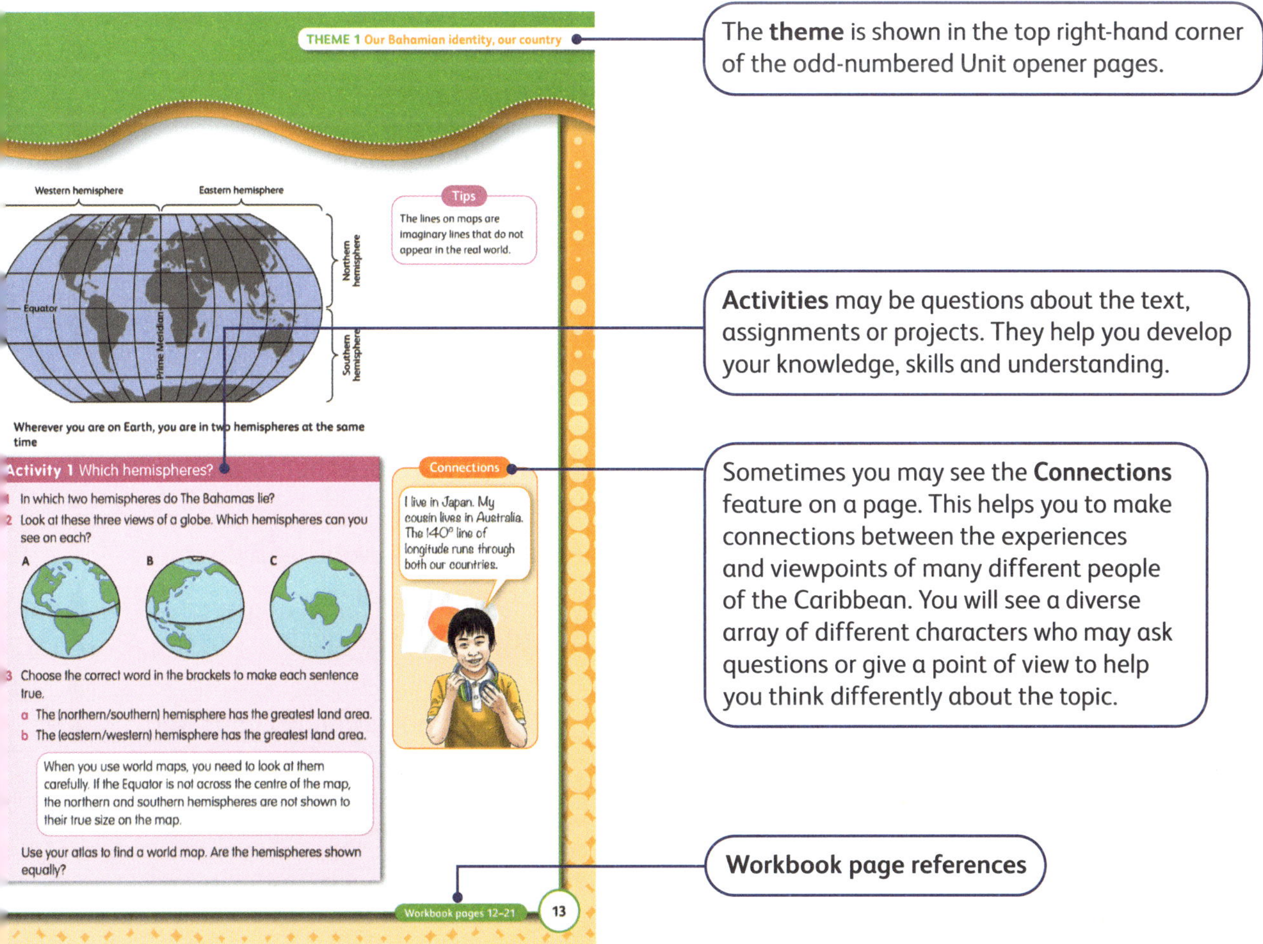


The **theme** is shown in the top right-hand corner of the odd-numbered Unit opener pages.

**Activities** may be questions about the text, assignments or projects. They help you develop your knowledge, skills and understanding.

Sometimes you may see the **Connections** feature on a page. This helps you to make connections between the experiences and viewpoints of many different people of the Caribbean. You will see a diverse array of different characters who may ask questions or give a point of view to help you think differently about the topic.

Workbook page references

# 1 National symbols and pride



## Our national symbols

**Word power**

symbol

Flags, Coats of Arms, mottoes and national anthems are all national **symbols**. Each country has its own national symbols that are important to the people of that country. National symbols often represent the country's history, and tell you what is important to people of that country and what they aim to achieve.

**March on, Bahamaland**

Lift up your head to the rising sun, Bahamaland;
March on to glory, your bright banners waving high.
See how the world marks the manner of your bearing!
Pledge to excel through love and unity.

Pressing onward, march together to a common loftier goal;
Steady sunward, tho' the weather hide the wide and treacherous shoal.
Lift up your head to the rising sun, Bahamaland,
'Til the road you've trod lead unto your God,

March on, Bahamaland!

▶ The flag, Coat of Arms and national anthem of The Bahamas are important national symbols

## Activity 1 Discuss our national symbols

1  How are national symbols important to the people of The Bahamas?

2  List three ways of showing respect for our national symbols.

3  Choose three of the symbols on our Coat of Arms. Explain the cultural or historical importance of each symbol.

4  When do we sing our national anthem?

5  What does our national motto on the Coat of Arms tell you about our values and what we hope to achieve as a nation?

## Activity 2 Compare flags of different countries

1  Our flag was designed by Rev. Dr Hervis L Bain and adopted on 10 July 1973.

   **a**  What is important about that date?

   **b**  What was our country's flag before that date? Why?

2  The colours on flags represent different things. What colour is used on our flag to represent:

   **a**  the strength and vigour of the people

   **b**  our maritime heritage and crystal clear waters

   **c**  sunshine and sandy beaches?

3  Which other countries in the Caribbean have blue and yellow on their flags?

4  Read the information below. Match each country to its flag.

- Japan and Switzerland both have a red and white flag. The red on the Japanese flag represents the rising sun.

- The flag of Brazil has 27 stars on a blue background. These represent states and districts in the country. The green on the flag represents the country's vegetation and forests.

- The South African flag represents the strength of the people using the same colour and shape as on our flag.

- The Australian flag also has stars on it. It includes a small British flag that represents its colonial past.

▶ **Flags from different countries**

# Who created our national symbols?

▲ Timothy Gibson

Our national symbols were developed to celebrate The Bahamas becoming an independent nation.

You already learnt that our national anthem *March on, Bahamaland* was written by Timothy Gibson, a composer and songwriter from Savannah Sound in Eleuthera. There is a monument in Savannah Sound that celebrates Timothy Gibson's life and work, and his contribution to nation building.

Our flag and Coat of Arms were designed by Dr Hervis L Bain from Nassau, New Providence. Dr Bain was an artist, a religious scholar, and a cultural icon. The short biographical note below, from a newspaper article, tells more about his life.

▲ Dr Hervis L Bain

### Reverend Doctor Hervis L Bain (1942–2015)

Dr Hervis Bain, a great cultural legend, made numerous outstanding contributions to the nation of The Bahamas.

As a nation builder, he welcomed a newly independent Bahamas onto the world stage in 1973 by creating our flag and the Coat of Arms. This gives him a special place in our national history.

Dr Bain was also an important figure in Education and Culture, and he had a particular interest in developing Junkanoo. His work influenced many other Bahamian nation builders.

## Activity 3 Write a short biographical note about a nation builder

1 Read the short article above about Dr Hervis Bain.
  a What does this tell you about Dr Bain?
  b Why is Dr Bain considered to be a nation builder? Give two reasons.
2 Do your own research to find out more about Timothy Gibson's life. Write a short biographical note like the one above about Timothy Gibson.

# Symbols past and present

Before The Bahamas became an independent nation in 1973, it was a colony of Britain (the United Kingdom). The flag and other symbols used at the time were closely linked to those of Britain.

For example, the British national anthem 'God Save Our Gracious Queen' was sung at national events and our flag contained the Union Jack and the seal of the Crown Colony of The Bahamas.

Today, our Coat of Arms (see page 6) is the official seal of our country. This means it is used to identify official documents (birth certificates, marriage certificates and passports) and other official items as belonging to The Bahamas.

▶ **The flag and the seal of the Crown Colony of The Bahamas**

## Activity 4 Compare the old and new seal of The Bahamas

1  The motto on the seal from colonial times is 'Expulsis piratis restituta commercia'.

   **a**  What does that mean?

   **b**  Why was that motto important historically?

2  Compare the colonial seal to our modern Coat of Arms.

   **a**  Can you find any similarities?

   **b**  Do you prefer the colonial seal or the modern Coat of Arms? Why?

## Activity 5 Design different symbols

1  Design a seal with a motto for your family. Draw and label it to show what the symbols represent.

2  Look closely at our modern Coat of Arms on page 6. What does the crown on the Coat of Arms represent?

3  **a**  How do you think the Coat of Arms of The Bahamas might change if our country became a republic and the monarch of the United Kingdom was no longer the head of state?

   **b**  Draw your ideas and share them with your group.

### Reflection

How and when did you learn the words of our national anthem?

How does singing the national anthem help us to feel proud to be Bahamian?

## National pride



**National pride** is when you love your country and feel proud of its history, culture and achievements. When you show national pride, you show that you are happy and excited to be a part of your country and want to show it off to others.

### Activity 6 How do we show national pride?

1 Discuss how these Bahamians are showing national pride.
2 Make a list of some other ways that citizens can display national pride in daily life and work.

## Be an ambassador

When we promote our country and culture, we are good **ambassadors** for The Bahamas. The people in the pictures are all good ambassadors, showing others they are proudly Bahamian.

**Word power**

ambassador

### Activity 7 Being a good ambassador for your country

1  Work with a partner. You will dramatise two situations in which a taxi driver picks up a tourist at the airport.
   - In the first role play, show how the taxi driver can be a poor ambassador for The Bahamas.
   - In the second role play, show how the taxi driver can be a good ambassador for The Bahamas.

2  You have been asked to teach the tour guides at a local chocolate factory how to be good ambassadors for The Bahamas.
   What would you tell them? Share your ideas as a class.

**In this unit, you will:**

- define the terms continent, country, hemisphere and Equator
- locate and label continents in different hemispheres
- locate The Bahamas
- identify and locate Japan, Brazil, Australia, Switzerland and South Africa.

## The Earth is divided into hemispheres

**Word power**

hemisphere
Equator

These pictures show two different ways of dividing an apple into halves.

The Earth cannot be cut into pieces like this, but it can be divided into imaginary halves. Half of the Earth is called a **hemisphere**.

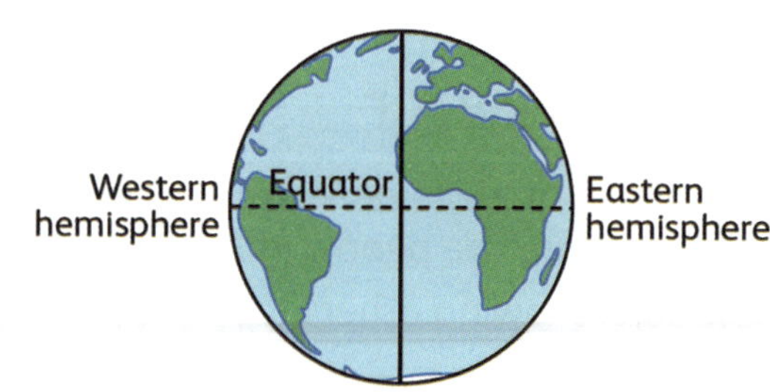


▲ **The Earth divided into hemispheres**

The **Equator** is the 0° line of latitude. It divides the Earth into the northern and the southern hemispheres.

If we divide the Earth along the 0° and the 180° lines of longitude, we get the eastern and western hemispheres. The 0° line of longitude is called the Prime Meridian and the 180° line of longitude is called the International Date Line. Places east of the Prime Meridian (up to the date line) are in the eastern hemisphere. Places west of the Prime Meridian (up to the date line) are in the western hemisphere.

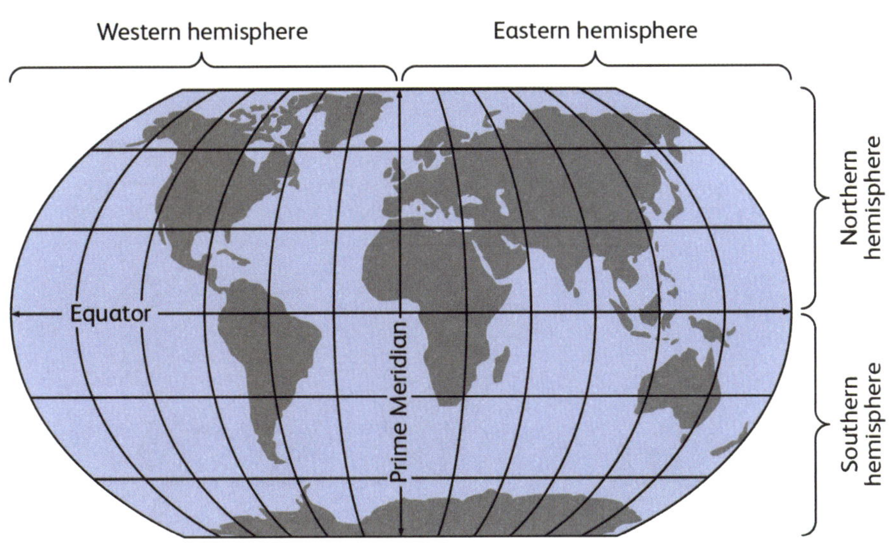


▲ **Wherever you are on Earth, you are in two hemispheres at the same time**

Activity 1 Which hemispheres?

1  In which two hemispheres do The Bahamas lie?

2  Look at these three views of a globe. Which hemispheres can you see on each?

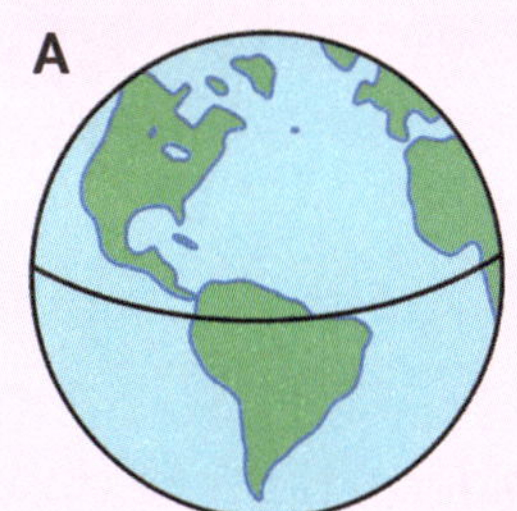


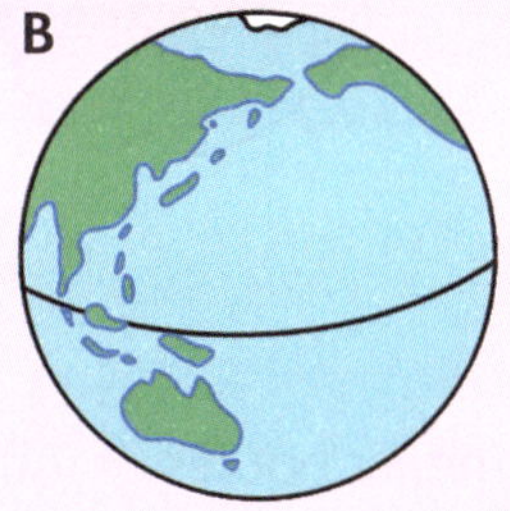


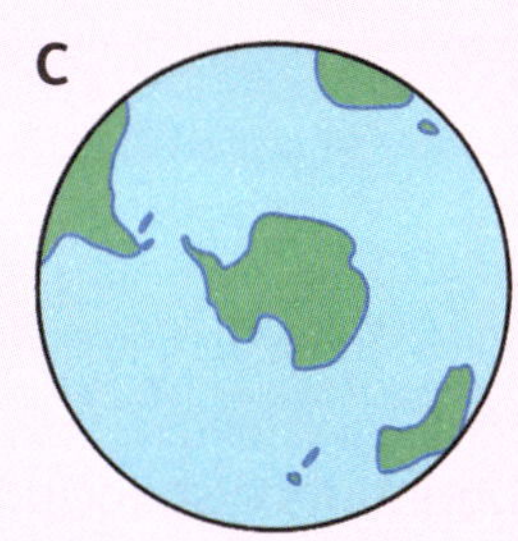


3  Choose the correct word in the brackets to make each sentence true.

   a  The (northern/southern) hemisphere has the greatest land area.

   b  The (eastern/western) hemisphere has the greatest land area.

4  When you use world maps, you need to look at them carefully. If the Equator is not across the centre of the map, the northern and southern hemispheres are not shown to their true size on the map.

   Use your atlas to find a world map. Are the hemispheres shown equally?

**Tips**

The lines on maps are imaginary lines that do not appear in the real world.

**Connections**

## Continents



**Continents** are the large bodies of land that make up the Earth. There are seven continents in the world: Africa, Asia, Antarctica, Australia, Europe, North America and South America. Europe and Asia are joined together and are sometimes called Eurasia.

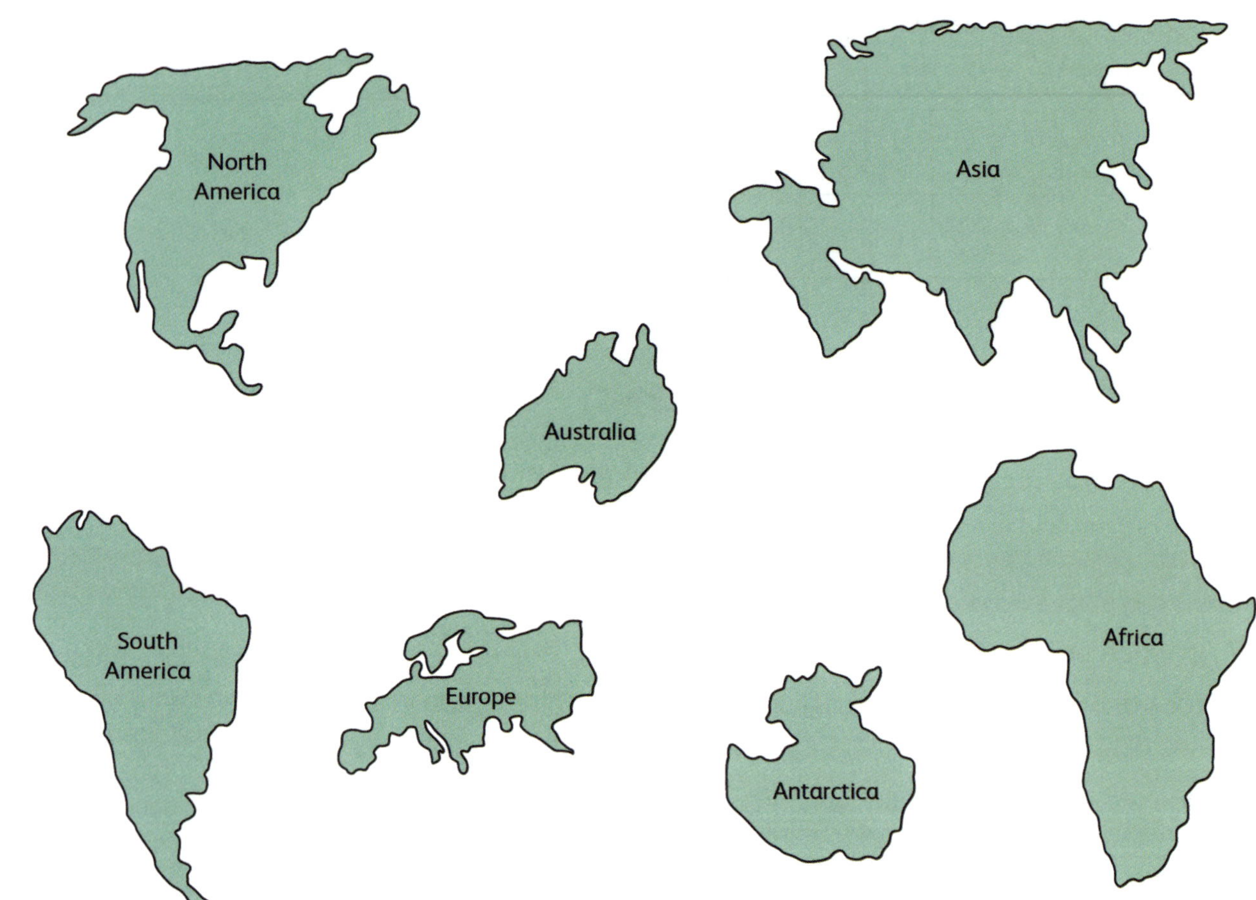


▲ **The seven continents**

**Tips**

The continents above are arranged in random order – in Activity 2, you will arrange them as they would appear on a world map.

Continents also include smaller bodies of land (islands) that are close to, but not always joined, to them. For example:

- Europe includes Iceland, the United Kingdom and Ireland.
- Australia, New Zealand and the island countries around Australia are included in the continent Australia, which is sometimes called Australasia or Oceania.
- The United Nations includes the countries in Northern America (Mexico, the USA, Canada and Greenland), the countries on the land bridge (Central America) and the Caribbean island nations as part of North America.
- Japan is part of Asia.

All of the continents (except Antarctica) are divided into different countries. A **country** is an independent nation with its own government.

## Activity 2 Make a world map

### You will need:

▶ scissors
▶ glue
▶ a ruler
▶ copies of the continent outlines
▶ a sheet of A4 paper
▶ coloured markers or crayons

1 Cut out the continents. Cut as close to their outlines as you can.
2 Arrange the continents as they would appear on a map of the world.
3 Divide your paper into hemispheres by folding it like this:

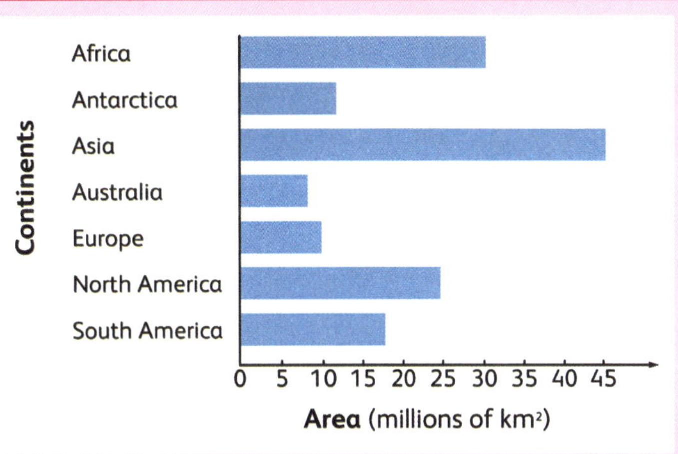

4 Now lay out the continents as they would appear on a world map. Make sure you have their names written on them. Glue them in place once you have decided where they should go.
5 Use your atlas to help you. Draw and label:
   a the Equator and Prime Meridian
   b the important island countries that are part of each continent.
6 Use your map to answer these questions. Which continents:
   a are located in the northern hemisphere
   b are located in the southern hemisphere
   c have parts in both the northern and southern hemispheres
   d are fully in the western hemisphere?

## Activity 3 Compare the size of continents

The graph shows the approximate area of each continent.

1 Use the data on the graph to write the names of the continents in order from smallest to greatest.
2 Write the area of each continent next to its name.



## Activity 4 Locate countries on different continents

1 Use your atlas if you need it to help you find and name these countries on your map.
   a Japan   b Brazil   c Australia   d Switzerland   e South Africa.
2 What is the capital of each country? List the names of the countries and their capitals.
3 Kesia says Australia is a continent. Rayshawn says it is a country. Explain why they are both correct.
4 Which continent do you know most about? How did you learn about it?
5 Which continent do you know least about? How could you find out more about it?

## Oceans and other bodies of water

Continents occupy about one quarter of the space on Earth. The rest of the Earth is covered by water. The large bodies of salt water between and around the continents are called **oceans**.

There are five oceans. The Pacific Ocean is the largest in area, followed by the Atlantic Ocean, Indian Ocean, Southern Ocean and Arctic Ocean.

**Word power**

- ocean
- sea
- gulf
- island
- coastline
- landlocked

### Activity 5 Locate the oceans on the world map

1 Find the oceans on a globe or a map of the world.
2 Add labels to your own map to show where each ocean is found.
3 The Southern Ocean is sometimes called the Antarctic Ocean. Suggest why.

▲ **The Gulf of Mexico and the Caribbean Sea**

A smaller part of an ocean that is close to land is called a **sea**. When the sea extends far into the land, it is called a **gulf**. For example, in our region, you can find the Caribbean Sea and the Gulf of Mexico, as shown on this map.

You already know that you live on an **island**. Islands are smaller than continents and they are surrounded by water. The Bahamas is an island nation. So are Japan and New Zealand.

Countries that share a boundary with a gulf, sea or ocean have a **coastline**. Countries that are surrounded by other countries are called **landlocked** countries. These countries do not have a coastline.

**Reflection**

How did working through this unit improve your knowledge of the world? Give two ways.

### Activity 6 Classify countries

Work with a partner. You will need your atlas.

1 Sort the countries in the box into two groups: landlocked countries and islands.

| | | | | | |
|---|---|---|---|---|---|
| Iceland | Bolivia | Sri Lanka | Cuba | Switzerland | Zambia |
| Mauritius | Mali | Cyprus | Greenland | Niger | Paraguay |

2 For each island, write the name of the sea or ocean in which is found and its capital city.
3 For each landlocked country, write the name of its capital city and the names of its neighbouring countries.

# 3 Working with different types of maps

> **In this unit, you will:**
> - use latitude and longitude to locate countries
> - learn about political and physical maps
> - work with maps to find out more about the political and physical features of different countries.

## Lines of latitude and longitude

You already know that lines of **longitude** are imaginary lines that run from north to south on the Earth. They are also called meridians. Longitude is measured in degrees east and west of the Prime Meridian (0°). When you write longitude, you need to add E or W to show which hemisphere you are in. The Bahamas is located between 71°W and 80°W. Australia is located between 112°E and 154°E.

Lines of **latitude** are the imaginary lines that run from east to west on the Earth. The Equator is the main line of latitude (0°) and other lines are numbered in degrees north and south of the Equator. When you write latitude, you add N or S to show which hemisphere you are in.

To give the location of a place, we first give the line of latitude closest to it, then we give the line of longitude closest to it. These two numbers are called **coordinates**. When writing coordinates, the degree symbols can be left out.

**Word power**

longitude
latitude
coordinates

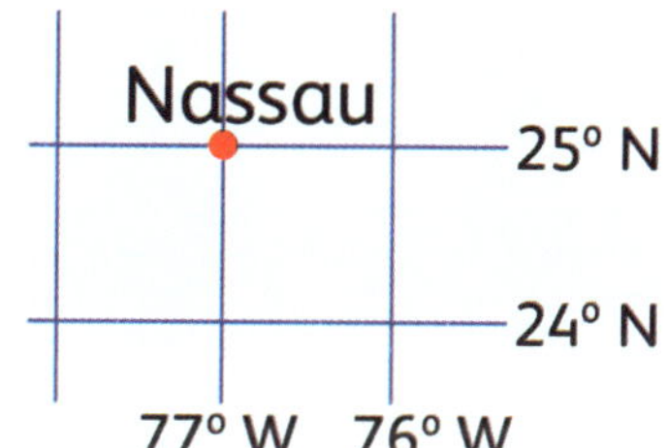


▲ The coordinates for Nassau are 25 N 77 W

**Did you know?**

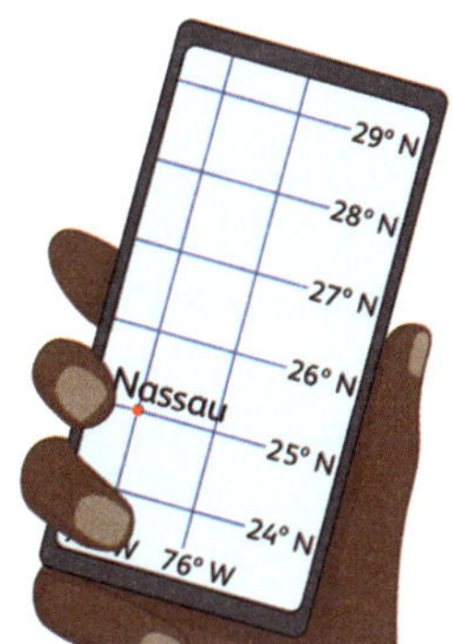


Today you can use mapping apps on a phone or computer to find the location of any place in the world, including its precise coordinates.

### Activity 1 Locate places using latitude and longitude

1  You are studying five countries: Japan, Brazil, South Africa, Australia and Switzerland. Work out which country you would find at each of these coordinates:

   a  30 S 135 E      b  30 S 45 W      c  30 S 25 E

   d  47 N 10 E       e  47 N 135 E.

2  Explain how you can work out which hemispheres a country is in by looking at the coordinates.

3  Write the names of the five countries. Next to each country, write its capital city. Give the latitude and longitude coordinates of these cities.

4  Find out about the location app '*What3words*'. Use it to find the three words that give the location of your school.

## Political and physical maps

If you look through your atlas, you will see that it has different kinds of maps. The maps are designed to give you different information about places.

**Political maps** show the human-made features of places. These include international and other boundaries, country names and labelled dots or other symbols to show towns and cities.

**Physical maps**, like the second map after the activity, show natural features like rivers, lakes, deserts, mountains, seas and oceans. Many physical maps use different colours to show the shape and height of the land. Most physical maps do not show boundaries between countries as they focus on natural features.

Basic political features like country names, some boundaries and the position of cities or towns are often shown on physical maps to make them clearer.

> **Word power**
>
> political map
> physical map

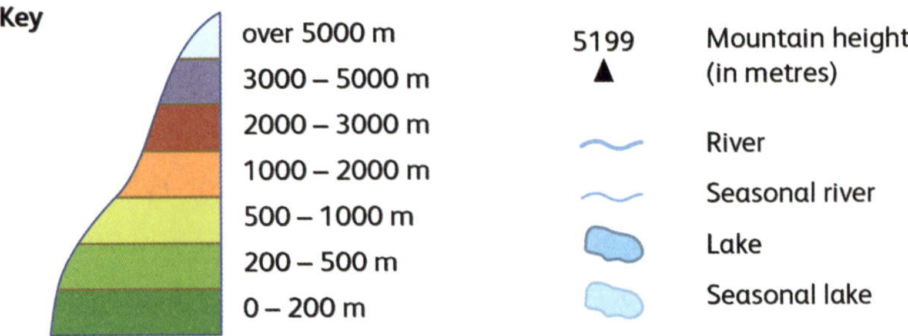


▲ The key on a physical map is important. It tells you what the colours and other symbols or shading represent

> **Connections**
>
> 
> 

### Activity 2 Compare political and physical maps

1 Look at the political map on the next page.
  a How are international boundaries shown on the map?
  b What symbol is used to show capital cities?
2 Find and write the name of the capital city of:
  a Haiti    b Belize    c Guyana    d Mexico.
3 Look at the map of Cuba on the next page.
  a What colour is used to show the highest land?
  b Which part of Cuba is the most mountainous?
  c Is it accurate to say that most of Cuba is less than 200m above sea level? Why or why not?
  d How can you tell whether the sea is shallow or deep on this map?
  e Explain why this map is not a purely physical map.

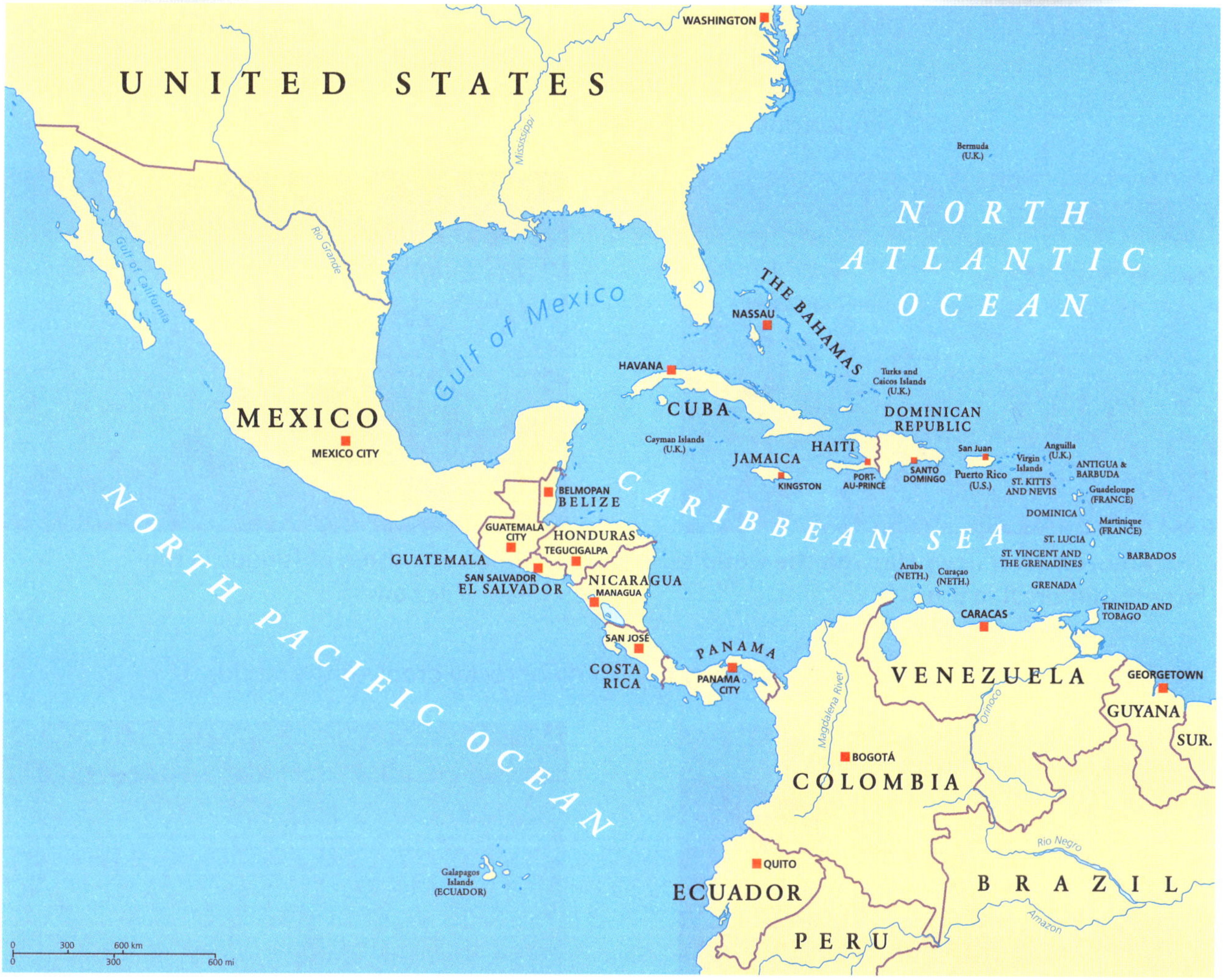


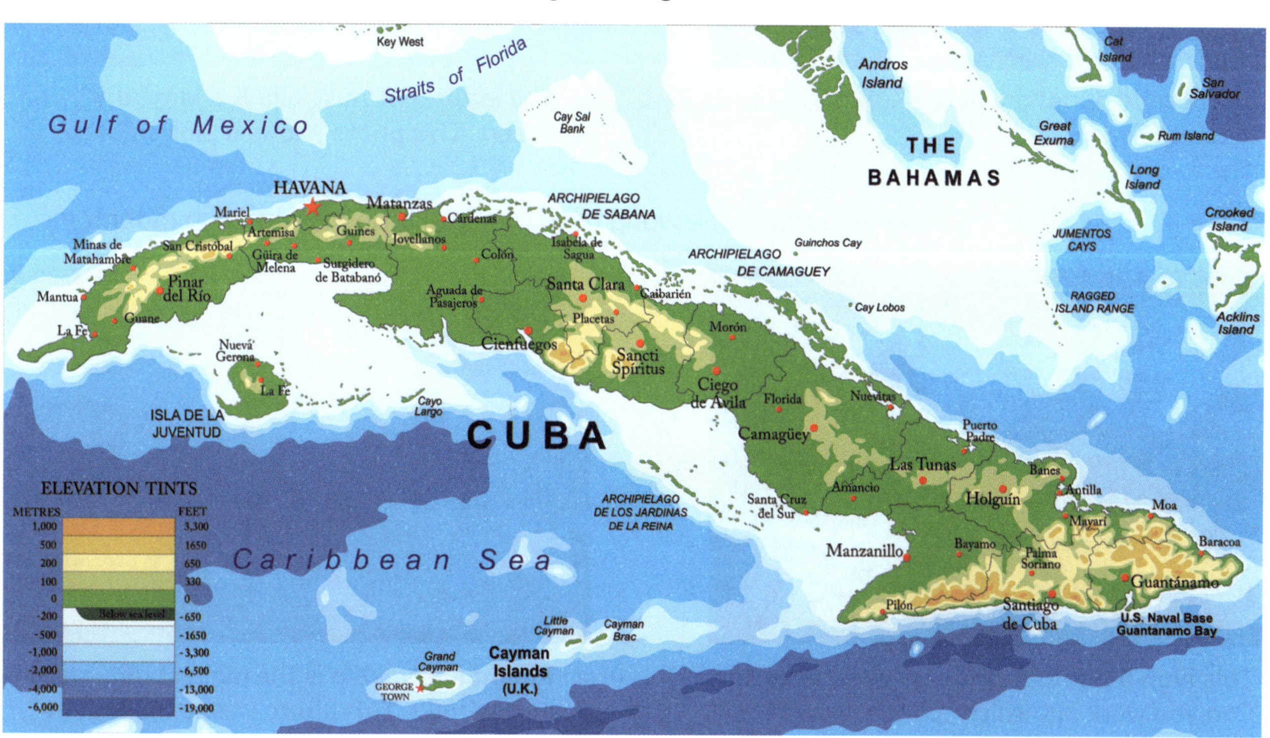

▲ A political map of the Caribbean and neighbouring countries

▲ A physical map of Cuba and the surrounding bodies of water

Workbook pages 22–31

# Physical features of different countries

Rivers and other large bodies of water, deserts and mountains are all important physical features.

▲ The Amazon River flows through the world's largest rainforest in Brazil

▲ Japan is a chain of islands in the Sea of Japan

Deserts are very dry sandy or rocky areas of the world.

▲ These sand dunes are in the Kalahari Desert in South Africa

▲ The interior of Australia is a large dry desert. This photo shows a pink salt lake

Some parts of the world have mountain ranges with high mountains.

▲ This high mountain range is called The Alps. Can you work out which country this is?

▲ Mount Kosciuszko is the highest mountain in Australia. This photo shows the Mount Kosciuszko National Park

## Activity 3 Find features on maps

You will need an atlas for this activity.

**1** List the pages in your atlas where you can find physical maps of Brazil, Japan, Australia, South Africa and Switzerland.

**2** The name of the longest river in each country is given below.

Murray    Shinano    Amazon    Rhine    Orange

  **a** Match each river to the country it is found in.

  **b** Write the river names in order from longest to shortest.

  **c** Draw a fun graph to compare the lengths of the rivers.

**3** Draw an outline map of Australia.

  **a** Colour the map to show the following deserts. Add a key to show what each colour means.

Gibson Desert    Simpson Desert    Great Victoria Desert

Tanami Desert    Great Sandy Desert

  **b** Estimate what percentage of Australia is desert.

**4** Find the Swiss Alps and the Australian Alps. Describe the location of each.

**5** Mount Fuji and Mount Aso are in Japan. Find them on the map and describe where each mountain is located.

## Activity 4 Make a display of the features of your island

Work in groups to make a large display map highlighting the main features and attractions of your island. You can include both natural features and built features.

- Plan carefully. Brainstorm ideas and do research to help you decide what to show on the map.

- Do some rough sketches of the map before you work on a large final version.

- Prepare your map and include labels and a key.

- Add fact sheets with photos or pictures to give information about some of the features you have included.

- Your teacher will tell you where to put up your finished display.

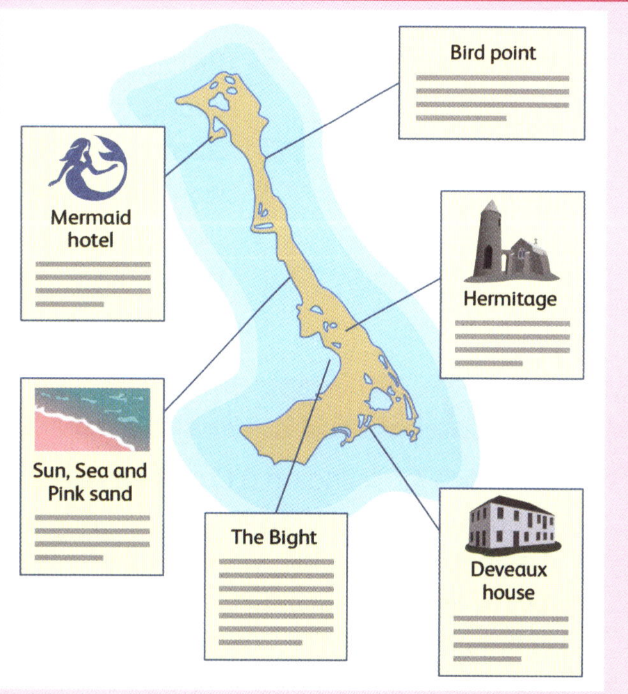

# 4 Natural disasters



## What is a natural disaster?

Natural hazards are events in nature that can be dangerous to people, animals or property. Examples of natural hazard are hurricanes, tsunamis, earthquakes and volcanic eruptions.

When a natural event causes damage to property and the environment and harms people, we call it a **natural disaster**. A hurricane in the middle of the ocean is a natural hazard, but if it makes landfall and damages property and leads to loss of life, it is a natural disaster.

People cannot stop natural hazards, but they can take steps to prepare for natural disasters. For example:

- In the Caribbean, we have hurricane tracking and warning systems, hurricane shelters and specialised emergency teams who act if there is a hurricane.
- In Japan, buildings are designed to withstand earthquakes, people take part in earthquake drills so they know what to do, and scientists monitor earth movement so they can send out alarms to warn people if there is an earthquake.
- In Australia, people clear bush and cut vegetation to make fire breaks to stop wildfires from spreading. They use a special smartphone app to get warnings and report fires.

**Word power**

natural disaster

## Activity 1 Describe natural disasters

1. Look at the sign found on a Caribbean beach.
   a. What two natural hazards does it warn people about? List these and explain what they are.
   b. How can knowing what to do help people in the event of a natural disaster?
2. What is the worst storm you have ever experienced? Write a short essay describing the storm and what happened.

# Regions with a high risk of natural disasters

The surface of the Earth is made of massive plates of solid rock. When these plates break or move suddenly, they release shockwaves that can cause earthquakes.

Breaking or moving plates can also force hot melted rock to the surface where it spills out as lava during a volcanic eruption. Many active volcanoes are found along cracks in the Earth's crust. Countries that are near cracks in the Earth's crust are more likely to experience earthquakes or experience a volcanic eruption.

This map shows the plates of the Earth's crust and a region called the Ring of Fire, where earthquakes and volcanoes are common.

**Connections**


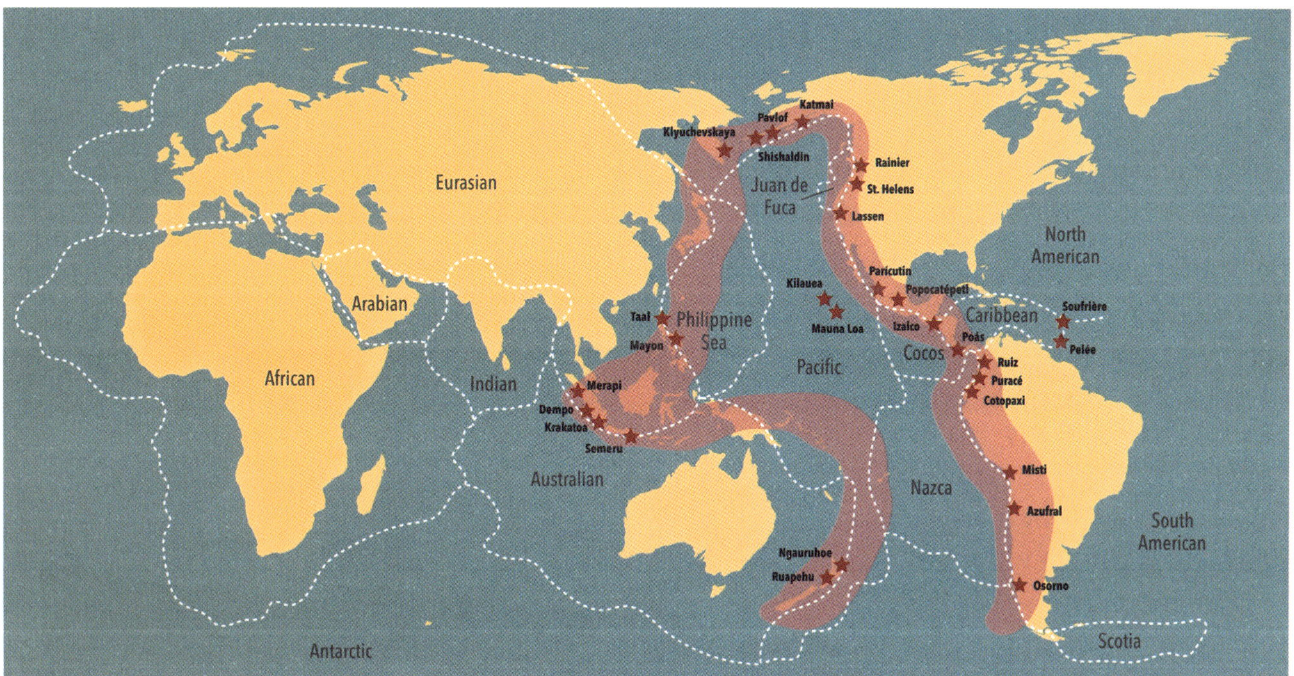


## Activity 2 Identify regions on a map

**1** Find the Caribbean Plate on the map above.
  **a** What does this tell you about our region?
  **b** Name the two active volcanoes to the east of the Caribbean Plate.
  **c** Use your atlas or search online to find the names of the islands where these volcanoes are.
**2** Describe the risk of an earthquake as low, medium or high for each of the countries below. Give reasons for your answers.
  **a** Australia      **b** South Africa      **c** Japan      **d** Brazil      **e** Switzerland
**3** In which of these five countries are you most likely to experience a volcanic eruption? Why?

## Case study

### Fukushima, Japan

In 2011, a powerful earthquake happened north-east of Japan. The earthquake caused a tsunami with waves up to 40 metres high. The tsunami hit the coast and wiped out almost everything in its path, including over 400,000 homes and many roads and bridges.

The earthquake and tsunami damaged a nuclear power plant called Fukushima Daiichi. The power supply failed and cooling systems for the nuclear reactors shut down. This caused explosions in the power plant. Radiation leaked into the air and the sea around the plant. More than 160,000 people who lived up to 20 km from the power station had to leave their homes because of the danger of radiation.

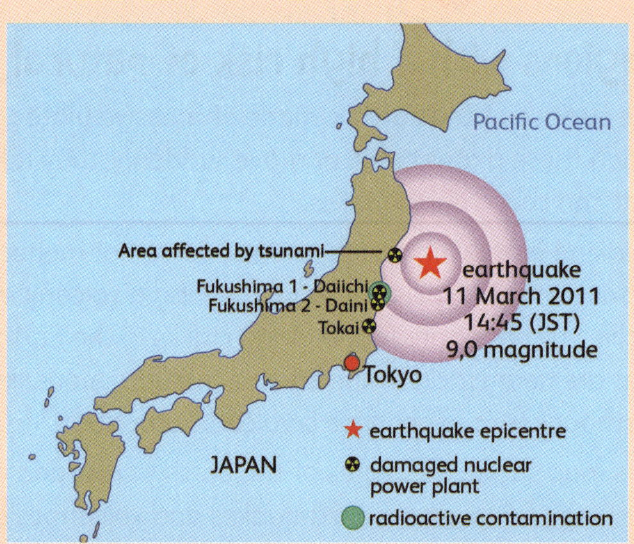


▲ **Location of the Fukushima earthquake**

The Japanese government and the power plant operators have been cleaning up the area and trying to make nuclear power plants safer. The clean-up operation involves removing soil, washing down buildings and roads, and cutting down trees in contaminated areas to make it safe for people to live there again. Some areas have been cleaned up and radiation levels are low enough for people to go back. Many people are still worried about the risk and have not returned to their old homes.

Cleaning up after a nuclear explosion takes a very long time. Experts say that the area affected by the Fukushima disaster will never be completely clean and safe.

In 2023, 12 years after the disaster, there were still some places where the radiation levels were too high for people to live safely. It is likely that dangerous radioactive materials from the disaster will stay in the environment for hundreds or thousands of years.

▲ **Many neighbourhoods along the coast were swept away by the massive waves**

## Activity 3 Discuss a case study

Read the case study on the previous page. Answer these questions with a partner.

1 Which two natural events led to the Fukushima disaster?
2 How was the natural disaster made much worse?
3 What is radioactive material and how can it harm living things?
4 How were people affected by these events?
5 What effects do you think these events had on the natural environment?
6 Explain why many people had still not returned to their old homes in 2023.

## Activity 4 Compare different regions

1 Match each country to the main types of natural hazards that it faces. You may need to do some research to work this out.

| Japan | Brazil | South Africa | Australia | Switzerland |
|---|---|---|---|---|
| Tropical cyclones, wild fires, floods and drought | Flooding and landslides and drought | Typhoons, tsunamis, earthquakes and volcanic eruptions | Tropical storms, droughts, floods, wildfires and tornadoes (rare) | Floods, rockfalls and avalanches and thunderstorms |

2 Choose one of the countries (other than Japan). Write a case study of a natural disaster that has affected that country. Provide a map, add pictures, and explain how the disaster affected people and the built and natural environment.

## Activity 5 Simulate a natural hazard

The United Nations Office for Disaster Risk Reduction has developed an online simulation game that you can play. It will help you to learn more about natural disasters and what people can do to prevent them or make their effects less serious. You can find the game online at www.stopdisastersgame.org.

Play the game and prepare a short talk for the class to summarise what you learnt from it.

The website www.sciencejournalforkids.org also has several simulation games that you can try and play if you are interested.

# Global warming and climate change

You may have heard about **climate change**. Climate change describes how the temperature and rainfall patterns of a region change over a long period of time.

Scientists have been keeping weather records for a long time. Their data shows that overall, the Earth is getting warmer. The rise in the overall temperature of the Earth is called **global warming**.

The rise in the temperature of the Earth has caused changes to climate patterns, known as climate change. Some places have become drier and others wetter. Cold places have become warmer and extreme weather events are more frequent. For example, stronger hurricanes happen more often, and also occur outside the hurricane season. Climate change is a hazard that affects the environment and the people who live in it.

The temperatures on Earth have always risen and fallen naturally. However, scientists agree that recently the temperature started increasing more quickly it would naturally. Human activities, such as farming, industry, vehicle exhaust fumes, burning fossil fuels and deforestation, release carbon dioxide and other gases (known as **greenhouse gases**) that trap heat in the Earth's atmosphere. Because there is so much carbon dioxide, plants cannot absorb it all. The carbon dioxide stays in the atmosphere where it absorbs heat.

Climate change affects the world's oceans. Scientists have discovered that sea levels are rising across the globe. This is partly because ice at the poles and in glaciers is melting and flowing into the oceans. Another reason is that water in the oceans is getting warmer – warm water expands and takes up more space. Rising sea levels are a hazard for island nations, including the countries in the Caribbean.

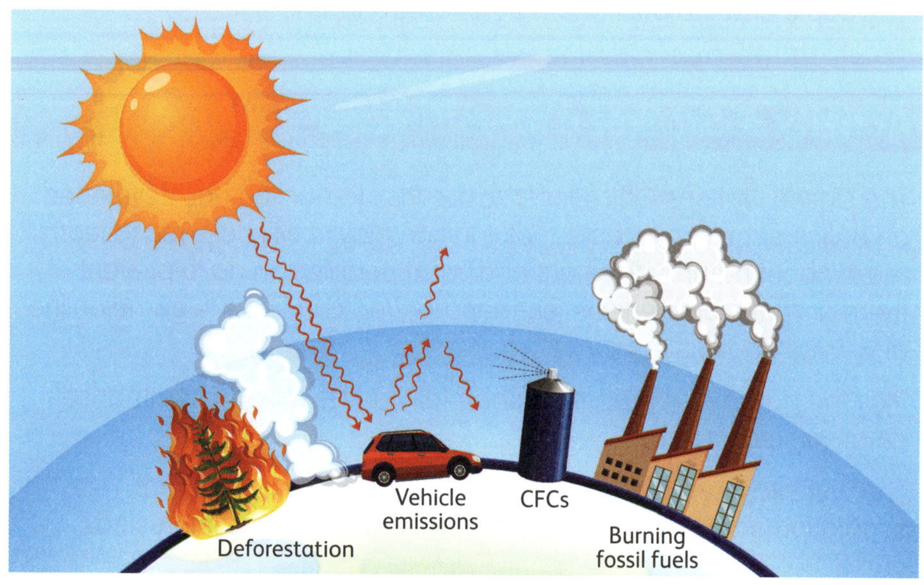


▶ **Causes of global warming**

## Activity 6 Research climate change and present your findings

Work in groups to create a digital or audio-visual presentation to teach children about global warming and climate change.

1 Before you start, think about where you can find accurate and up-to-date information.

2 Find the answers to these questions (you can split up the work among group members):

   a What are global warming and climate change?

   b What are the causes of climate change?

   c How do humans contribute to climate change?

   d How will climate change affect people and places?

   e Why is climate change a threat to the countries of the Caribbean?

   f What is the '1.5 to stay alive' project?

   g What can people do to reduce the effects of climate change?

3 Prepare your presentation.

4 Present your work to the class.

5 Give each other feedback. Ask questions and make suggestions for improving the presentation.

### Reflection

Read these statements. Decide whether each one is true or false.

- Climate change is not caused by humans.
- Droughts and floods are both effects of climate change.
- Global warming only affects people in cold countries.
- Glaciers are melting because of global warming.
- Climate change is good news because it means sunnier weather.
- We cannot do anything to reduce global warming.
- Even small changes can make a big difference.

# 5 Different forms of government



## Countries and their governments

**Word power**

government
executive
legislature
judiciary
Constitution

Independent states are countries that have their own **government**, justice system, security forces and public services. The Bahamas has all these institutions, so we are a sovereign or independent state.

The government is the organisation that runs a state and keeps law and order. Most governments have different branches performing different functions to run the country:

- The **executive** is the head of state and the ministries work with the head of state to run the country.
- The **legislature** is the group of people who make laws.
- The **judiciary** are the judges and courts that make sure the laws are obeyed and that the government itself upholds the **Constitution** of the country.

## Activity 1 Why do countries need a government?

1 Look at this imaginary country. It is an island with natural resources, with many people living there.

2 Discuss why the people in this country need some form of government. Think about:

  **a** rules and laws

  **b** providing and maintaining services such as water, electricity, health care, education, communication and transport

  **c** trade and relationships with other countries

  **d** ownership and use of natural resources.

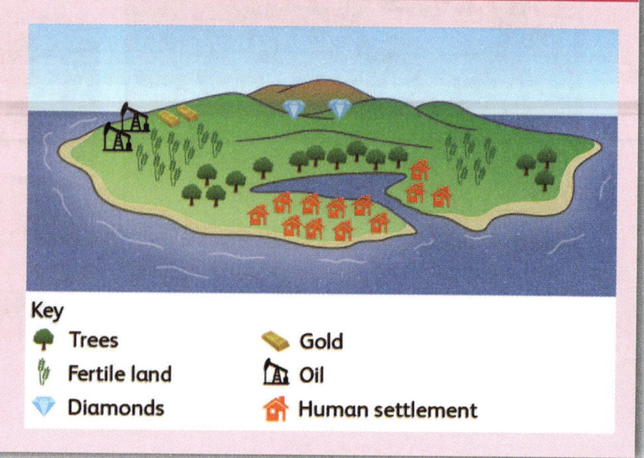

# Different forms of government

The characteristics of different forms of government are summarised in the table below.

**Word power**

monarchy   democracy
republic   dictatorship

| Form and structure of government | Examples |
|---|---|
| **Monarchy**<br>• The monarch (king, queen, emperor, sultan, sheikh) is head of state. The role of monarch is usually inherited and once a monarch is crowned, they normally rule for the rest of their life. Queen Elizabeth II of the United Kingdom reigned for over 70 years. Her son Charles became King Charles III after her death.<br>• In a parliamentary monarchy, the monarch is the ceremonial head of state only. They do not make or implement policy. The government of the country is carried out by the elected parliament. | • Saudi Arabia is a kingdom with a king.<br>• The Vatican City is a monarchy with the pope as its head of state.<br>• The Bahamas is a parliamentary monarchy – so is the United Kingdom and Australia.<br>• Japan is a parliamentary monarchy headed by an emperor. |
| **Democracy**<br>• In a democracy, the citizens of the state elect the leaders they want to represent them.<br>• In a parliamentary democracy, the parliament chooses the head of state and ministers. The political party with most votes usually leads the government.<br>• In a federal democracy, the power of government is split between a central government and the authorities of the different parts that make up the country as a whole. | • Most countries in the world today have some form of democracy.<br>• The Bahamas and South Africa are parliamentary democracies.<br>• The USA, Canada and Australia are federal democracies. |
| **Republic**<br>• Any state where the government is elected by the people and the president rules without a monarch is called a republic.<br>• The name of the country normally tells you whether it is a republic or not. | • South Africa is a republic.<br>• Brazil and Switzerland are federal republics.<br>• In 2023, 159 out of 197 countries in the world were republics. |
| **Dictatorship**<br>• In a dictatorship, one person or a small group of people rule the country with absolute power and usually without an election or Constitution.<br>• Some dictatorships are ruled by military force.<br>• Most countries under a dictator do not call themselves a dictatorship. | • North Korea is recognised as a military dictatorship.<br>• Some countries that are republics or democracies could in reality be dictatorships.<br>• In 2023, the United Nations listed 51 countries as dictatorships. |

## Activity 2 Research and compare forms of government

1  Carry out your own research to find out about the current government of the USA, Australia and Brazil.

   **a**  Complete a fact file, like this outline, for each country.

> **Fact file**
>
> Full name of the country: _______________________________
>
> Form of government: _______________________________
>
> Current head of state: _______________________________
>
> Year of last election: _______________________________
>
> Year of next election: _______________________________
>
> Main political parties: _______________________________

   **b**  All three of these countries have a federal system of government. What are the main differences between them?

2  Draw up a table to compare the forms of government found in Japan and Switzerland.

## Activity 3 What will the government do?

Work in a group.

1  Read the information and answer the questions that follow.

> A small deposit of minerals has been found in a national park. The minerals can be extracted, but the environment will be badly damaged and some endangered species will lose their habitat. The people who live in the area disagree about whether the minerals should be extracted or not.

2  How do you think this problem would be solved by the government of a:

   **a**  constitutional monarchy (such as The Bahamas)

   **b**  federal republic

   **c**  dictatorship?

## Activity 4 How can you be a leader at school?

1  If your school was a country, what type of government would it have? Give reasons for your answer.

2  What makes a good leader at school? Make your own display, like this example, to show what characteristics are important in a school leader.

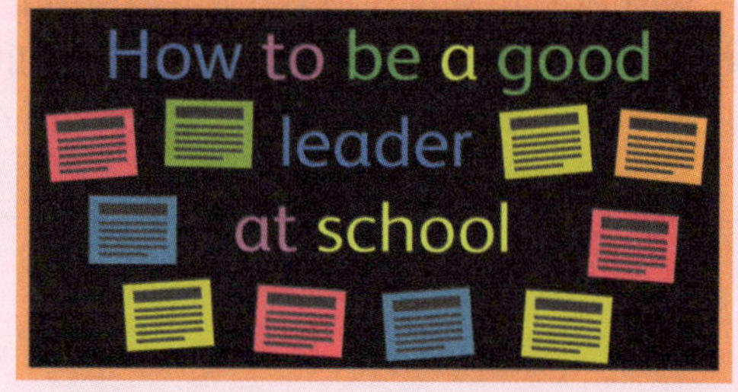

# Government and the Constitution

Most forms of government follow a set of agreed laws and principles contained in a Constitution. The Constitution is the highest law of the land; it outlines the system of government and defines the roles of the different parts of the government. The Constitution also lists the rights and responsibilities of the government and lists the rights that are guaranteed to citizens of the country.

Sometimes a Constitution may need to be amended (changed or corrected). Think about the Constitution of the USA – it became law in 1787. Since then, many things have changed. For example:

- In 1920, the US Constitution was amended to give all women the right to vote.
- In 1951, it was amended to limit the time a president could be in office to two terms.

The ways in which a Constitution may be changed (amended) are often explained in detail. The Constitution of The Bahamas may be amended by an Act of Parliament signed by both houses. In the past, our Constitution has been amended to:

- talk about men and women in places where it used to only specify men
- make it unlawful to discriminate against people based on their gender.

> **Reflection**
>
> There is a lot of information in this unit. How can you make sure you understand and remember it?

## Activity 5 Create a puppet show

Work with a partner to create a short puppet show that teaches young children:

- what a Constitution is
- why it is important for a country to have one.

## Activity 6 Can you say and do what you want?

1 Read this extract from our Constitution. Discuss what it means.

> '...every person in The Bahamas is entitled to the fundamental rights and freedoms of the individual, that is to say, has the right, whatever their race, place of origin, political opinions, colour, creed or sex, but subject to respect for the rights and freedoms of others and for the public interest ...'

2 What would you tell the person in the picture?

**In this unit, you will:**

- use the correct terms to outline and sequence the election process
- explain the role of the Governor-General, the government and the opposition in our constitutional monarchy
- identify the three branches of government and the organisations responsible for making laws
- explain the process of a bill becoming a law using the correct terms.

## Electing the government

**Word power**

election

In a democracy, adult citizens vote in **elections** to choose the people or political parties they want to represent them.

The Constitution of The Bahamas states that a general election must be held at least once every five years, but the Prime Minister can call an election at any time. The results of a general election determine which party will govern until the next election.

### Activity 1 Find out about the present government

1 Find out which parties are represented in parliament.
2 Which party is the ruling party? How many seats do they have in parliament?
3 Who are the opposition? How many seats does the opposition have in parliament?

### Activity 2 Why is it important to vote?

1 Read what different people say about voting in an election.

(Continued)

**2** Write a short paragraph explaining why it is important to vote in an election.

## The steps in the election process

The first step in the election process involves **dissolving** the government. The Prime Minister advises the Governor-General to dissolve parliament.

Once parliament is dissolved, the Prime Minister calls for an election and announces when the **election day** will be. The law says that the election must be announced at least 17 days before it happens, but the time between the announcement and the election is usually much longer so that everyone has a fair chance to prepare.

Any independent person or political party who intends to stand for election must file **nomination** papers to run for office. There is usually a date by when this must happen and all nominees pay a deposit which is only refunded to them if they get a minimum share of the votes.

Between the announcement and the election day, the different parties try to convince people to vote for them. The parties carry out a **campaign** to tell people what they stand for and what they will do if they are elected. A campaign usually includes posters, home visits and mass rallies.

> **Word power**
>
> dissolving
> election day
> nomination
> campaign

## Activity 3 Create your own campaign poster

Work in groups.

1  Choose an issue that is important to you and that would make life better for everyone in your community.
2  Work together to make a campaign poster that will help to convince people to vote for your group so that they can do something about this issue.
3  Include a name for your group, a catchy slogan, what you promise to do if you are elected, and at least one reason why people should vote for your group.

**Word power**

ballot

On election day, all registered voters go to their local polling station to cast their votes on specially printed forms, called **ballots**. Casting a vote is done in an enclosed booth so that a person's vote remains secret. Schools, church halls and other public buildings are used as polling stations. Once voting closes, the votes are tallied and counted, and the winners in each constituency are announced.

The results of the election tell us how many people from each party will become members of parliament. The party with the most members of parliament become the ruling party.

## Activity 4 Read a table of results

Read this table of election results.
Answer the questions.

1  How many votes were counted in total?
2  How many parties took part in the election?
3  Which party won most of the votes? How many votes did they get?
4  In order to get your nomination deposit back, you have to get at least $\frac{1}{8}$ of the total votes. Did the party with the fewest votes get their deposit back?

| Results of national election | |
|---|---|
| **Party** | **Number of votes** |
| Yellow Party | 335 087 |
| Blue Party | 214 099 |
| Green Party | 113 456 |
| Sleepy Party | 23 765 |

## Activity 5 Draw a flowchart of the electoral process

1  Draw a flowchart to summarise the steps in the electoral process.
2  Discuss in groups how you can remember the order of the steps.

## Forming a government

The government of The Bahamas is a constitutional monarchy. The king of the United Kingdom is the ceremonial head of state. The Governor-General is the king's representative in parliament. He or she presides over the government.

Within a few days of the election, the Governor-General swears in the new Members of Parliament (the winning candidates from each constituency) and appoints the leader of the ruling party as Prime Minister. The Governor-General also appoints and swears in the members of the Senate. Senators are not elected members of parliament, although the Governor-General takes advice on who should be in the senate from the ruling party and the opposition.

After everyone in parliament has been sworn in, the Governor-General invites the Prime Minister to form the new government.

## The structure of our government

The diagram below shows the three branches of government. Refer back to this diagram as you learn more about the functions of the three branches in the section that follows.

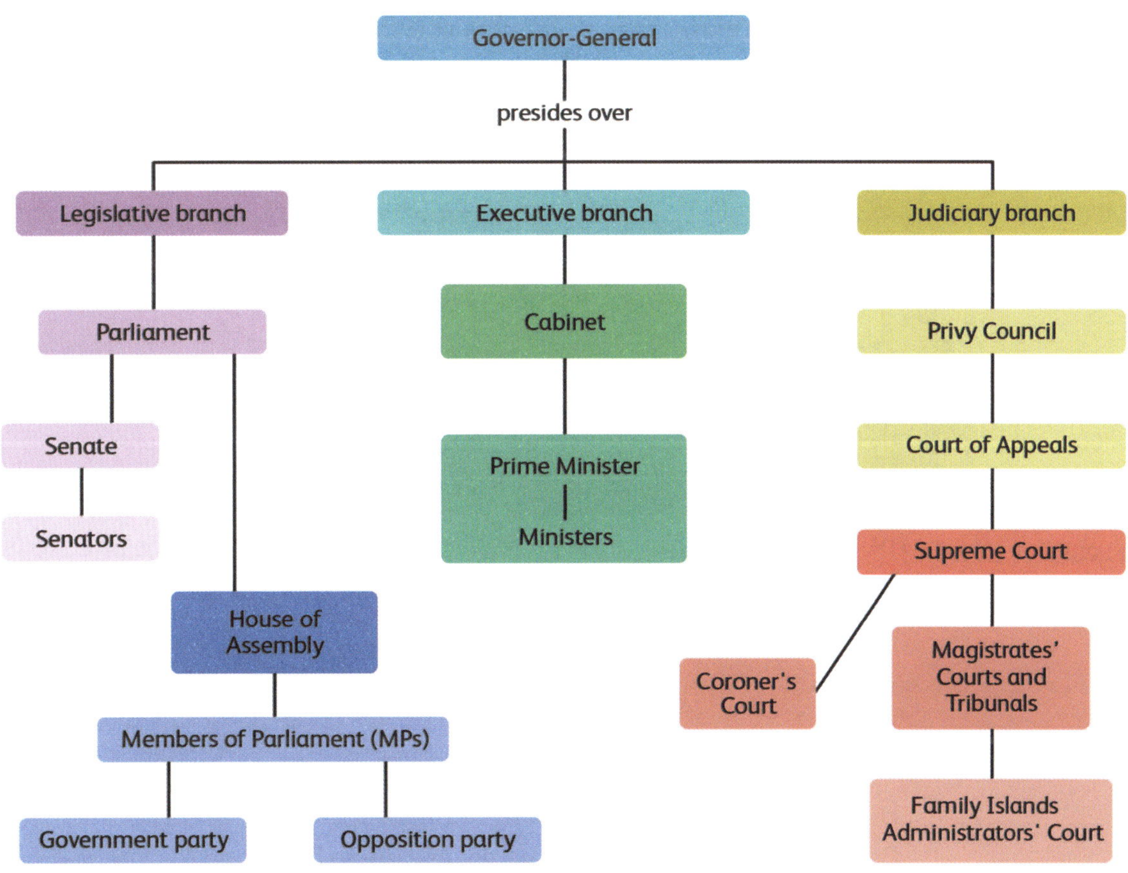

# What does each branch of government do?

The three branches of government work together to run the country and deal with national issues.

## The legislative branch

The legislative branch of government is also called the parliament.

There are two houses of parliament:

- The House of Assembly consists of elected Members of Parliament (MPs) from the government party and the opposition.
- The Senate consists of senators appointed by the Governor-General. Both houses play a role in the parliament.

The parliament is responsible for writing and passing laws, called **Acts of Parliament**, which must be followed by the whole country. To make sure that laws are just and fair to everyone, they are debated and discussed in detail by the Members of Parliament before they are signed into law.

> **Word power**
>
> Act of Parliament

The parliament is also responsible for making decisions about how to raise and spend the money needed to run our country. Money must be budgeted to pay for health services, education, transport, tourist services and many other things the country needs. The parliament must decide how to raise this money and how much of it should come from taxes on companies and individuals.

The members of the House of Assembly elect a Speaker. The Speaker's role is to preside over debates and make sure that parliamentary sessions run smoothly.

---

### Activity 6 Act out a debate in the House of Assembly

Work in groups to act out a debate.

Elect a Speaker to manage your debate.

Debate whether taxes on businesses should be raised for the next year. Decide who will be against the motion and who will support it before you start.

## The executive branch

The executive branch of government is called the Cabinet. The Cabinet makes sure the laws made by parliament are carried out.

The Cabinet must have at least 9 members, including the Prime Minister and the Attorney-General. Other members of the cabinet are called Ministers. Each minister heads up a separate ministry that is responsible for a particular area of the government's work.

In our Cabinet, ministers may come from the House of Assembly or from the Senate. Both the Prime Minister and the Minister of Finance must be Members of Parliament. No more than three ministers may be chosen from the Senate.

▲ Cabinet sometimes meets with other agencies. For example, during a hurricane, the cabinet will meet with members of the National Emergency Management Agency (NEMA) to discuss plans to deal with the effects of the hurricane

### Activity 7 Find out about the work of different ministries

Find out more about these four ministries:

- Ministry of Health and Wellness
- Ministry of Transport and Housing
- Ministry of Tourism, Investment and Aviation
- Ministry of Agriculture, Marine Resources and Family Island Affairs

1 Find out the name of the Minister in charge.
2 Describe the work of the Ministry.
3 How does the Ministry help to develop our country?

**Tips**

Most government ministries now have a website that gives you information about the officials and their work.

# The judiciary

You already know that the parliament makes the laws for our country. The judiciary is the branch of government that interprets the laws, hears and resolves disputes, and applies the Constitution in the name of the state. The judicial authority of The Bahamas is vested in the system of courts, as well as in the judges and magistrates who sit in these courts.

### Reflection

Flowcharts are useful to show some types of information.

What types of information are suitable to be shown in flowcharts? Why?

▲ **The Supreme Court Building in Nassau and the seal of the court**

### Connections

### Word power

bill

debate

### Activity 8 Draw a flowchart of how bills become laws

1 Read the information carefully. Then draw a flowchart to show the process that a bill goes through to become a law.

Both chambers of parliament are involved in writing, discussing and passing laws.

The first step in passing a law is introducing and reading a bill in the House of Assembly. A **bill** is a draft proposal that will be debated, changed, and voted on before it becomes law.

Each bill is read three times in the House of Assembly. The House members **debate** the bill in detail and make sure all parts of it are clear and acceptable before they vote to pass it or not.

If the House members vote to accept the bill after the third reading, it goes to the Senate. The same process is followed in the Senate. If the Senate votes to change the bill, it goes back to the House for approval. Once the Senate votes to approve the bill, it goes to the Governor-General for signature.

The power of the Senate is limited by the Constitution. If the Senate rejects a bill that has been approved twice by the House, the bill may be sent to the Governor-General for signing without Senate approval. A bill only becomes law once the Governor-General has signed it. It is then called an Act of Parliament.

2 Explain why laws are important for a well-functioning society.

# 7 Law enforcement

> **In this unit, you will:**
> - identify the types of courts found in The Bahamas and distinguish between them
> - define the terms defendants, jury, constable and justice of the peace
> - describe the roles of the Family Island Administrators and the local Board of Works.

## The courts uphold the law

Some laws apply to our rights, such as the right to vote and the right to express yourself freely. Other laws apply to how everyone is expected to behave. For example, it is against the law to steal somebody else's belongings, and also to drink alcohol and then drive a car. When people disobey laws, they commit a crime. Some crimes are considered more serious than others. For example, murdering someone is much more serious than stealing a handbag.

When someone is caught or suspected of breaking the law, they are arrested by the police. The police do not decide whether the person is guilty of the crime or not – that is the job of the court. People who are accused of crimes must appear in court. It is up to the court to hear evidence and decide whether the person is guilty or not. If the person is found guilty, the court decides what their punishment will be.

### Activity 1 What happens in a court?

1 Look at the picture of a court scene. Answer the questions.
   a Who is the defendant in this court?
   b The person passing sentence is an official of the court. What do we call these officials?
   c Do you think the defendant committed a very serious crime? Give a reason for your answer.
   d Defendants in a court case have to swear that they will tell the truth. Why do you think this is important? What happens if they do not tell the truth?

2 Have you ever watched a court scene in a film or series? Tell your group about it and what happened.

# Different courts to deal with different issues

There are different kinds of courts that deal with different types of offences and legal issues.

## Magistrate's courts

These are courts that deal with minor offences, such as petty theft and damage to property. Magistrate's courts also deal with civil matters such as speeding, drunk driving and disagreements between individuals.

A **magistrate** presides over the court. The magistrate hears the evidence and decides whether the **defendant** is guilty or not. If the defendant is guilty, the magistrate decides what the punishment will be. This could be community service, a fine or a short prison sentence.

## Family Island Administrators

On the Family Islands, there are Administrators' courts that deal with minor offences. The Administrator is the chief government representative on the island and they act as the judge in these courts. They are assisted in law enforcement by local police officers (**constables**) and local **Justices of the Peace** who have the same powers as a magistrate to sign and issue warrants. They may also be assisted by the local Board of Works.

## The Supreme Court

The Supreme Court is the second-highest court within court. This court has the power to hear any legal or criminal case, no matter how much money is involved, how serious the crime is or how complicated the case is. This means that everyone can go to the Supreme Court for help, no matter how big or small their problem is.

The Supreme Court can make decisions about what the Constitution means and can interpret the meaning of different laws. Supreme Court decisions must be followed by all the other courts in The Bahamas.

The Supreme Court is presided over by the Chief Justice and a bench of Justices appointed by the Governor-General. Criminal cases in the Supreme Court are heard in front of a **jury**. The jurors are ordinary men and women who are asked to listen to the evidence before they vote on whether the person is guilty or not.

> **Word power**
>
> magistrate
> defendant
> constable
> Justice of the Peace
> jury

▲ **Supreme Court Justices in front of the court**

## Activity 2 Act as a jury

Work in small groups. Imagine you have been chosen to be jurors in a Supreme Court trial.

The defendant has been accused of stealing millions of dollars in a festival ticket scam. The prosecution alleges that the defendant sold tickets online for a festival that did not exist. The defendant pleads not guilty. He says the festival was cancelled and the ticket money was paid to suppliers – he did not steal it.

1. What evidence do you think you would hear during the trial?
2. How would you decide whether the defendant was guilty or not guilty? Discuss this as if you are the jurors.
3. If the defendant is guilty, what type of punishment do you think would be fair for this crime? Give reasons for your answers.

## The Court of Appeals

The Court of Appeals is the highest court within The Bahamas. It is headed by a president who is assisted by a team of justices.

When someone feels they have been treated unfairly in a magistrate's court or the Supreme Court, or that the law was not properly applied, they may lodge an appeal. The bench of the Court of Appeal meets and decides whether the appeal is successful or not, based on the Constitution and the relevant laws.

**Reflection**

How can you remember which court does what? Write two things you will do to help you.

## Activity 3 Interview a justice

Imagine you are going to interview a justice from the Court of Appeals. Write a list of five questions that you would ask during the interview.

## The Privy Council

The highest court within The Bahamas is the Court of Appeals. If an issue cannot be decided by that court, it may be taken to the Privy Council. This is a special appeals court in England which can decide matters for constitutional monarchies under the King of England. For example, the Privy Council ruled in 2006 that it was unconstitutional for a person in The Bahamas to get a compulsory death sentence when convicted of murder.

**Word power**

unconstitutional

## Activity 4 Research the Juvenile Court

1. Find out what the Juvenile Court is and does.
2. Persons under the age of 18 may not be sent to prison. Find out where juvenile offenders are sent if they need to be detained.

## Activity 5 Draw a flowchart

Draw a flowchart to show the ranking of the courts in our legal system. Start with the lowest courts.

## Theme 1 What have you learnt?

### Unit 1 National symbols and pride

1 Choose one of the national symbols of The Bahamas. Write a short paragraph describing it and explaining its importance and use.

2 Choose one other country you studied in this unit. Sketch its flag and write short notes to explain what the colours or symbols on the flag represent.

### Unit 2 Continents and oceans

Look at this map and answer the questions:

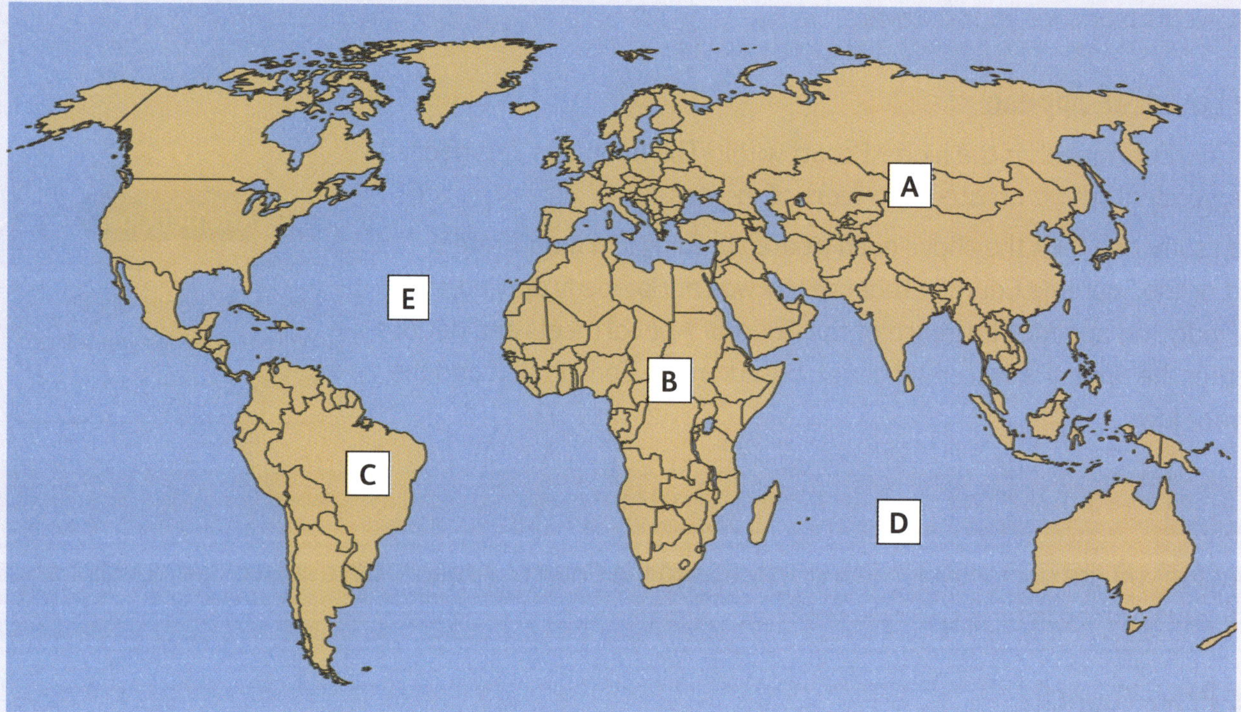


3 **a** Name the continents A, B and C.

  **b** Which oceans are at D and E?

4 Which continent is The Bahamas considered to be a part of?

5 Which continent is both an island and a country?

6 Name the ocean that is located west of North and South America.

7 On which continent do the fewest people live? Why?

### Unit 3 Working with different types of maps

8 Sketch two maps of an imaginary island to show the difference between a physical and political map.

9 Write a set of instructions for using latitude and longitude to locate places on a map.

## (Continued)

### Unit 4 Natural disasters

**10** Name the natural disaster that involves:

   **a** hot lava flowing out onto the Earth's surface

   **b** a very strong storm with swirling winds

   **c** rock or snow slipping down a mountain

   **d** violent shaking of the Earth due to plate movement

   **e** a really massive wave caused by shock waves under the ocean.

**11** Droughts and floods are happening more often in many different parts of the world. Scientists link this to climate change. Write a short paragraph explaining what climate change means.

**12** Why does climate change present a serious threat to countries of the Caribbean?

### Unit 5 Different forms of government

**13** What is the difference between a democracy and a dictatorship?

**14** Which of these countries has a similar system of government to The Bahamas?

   **a** Japan      **b** The United Kingdom      **c** Cuba

   **d** Russia      **e** Australia

**15** What is the title of the head of these types of monarchies?

   **a** an empire      **b** a kingdom      **c** an emirate

**16** What is the highest law in a constitutional democracy? Explain how this law protects the rights of every citizen.

### Unit 6 Electing and forming a government

**17** Write a definition for each term:

   **a** election      **b** opposition

   **c** nomination form      **d** campaign

**18** Put these steps in the election process into the correct order.

| | |
|---|---|
| nomination | government formed |
| election day announcement | election day |
| campaigning | nomination election date announcement |
| dissolution of parliament | swearing in |

**19** What is the role of the Governor-General in the electoral process?

### Unit 7 Law enforcement

**20** Match the type of court to the issues it deals with.

| | |
|---|---|
| Supreme Court | Local issues on Family Islands |
| Court of Appeal | Serious offences like murder or bank robbery |
| Privy Council | Traffic offences and petty theft |
| Administrator's Court | Criminal appeals from the Supreme Court |
| Magistrate's Court | Unresolved appeals and constitutional issues |

**In this unit, you will:**

- define and use the terms Constitution, citizens, independence and constitutional reform
- state how the Constitution defines citizenship and outline how a person may become a citizen
- compare the Constitution of The Bahamas with those of other countries
- revise the process of making laws
- describe the work of customs agencies and the prison service in enforcing laws.

## The Constitution and the right to citizenship

You already know that the Constitution is the highest law of our country. All other laws must follow the rules set out in the Constitution.

Any law that goes against the rules set out in the Constitution is unconstitutional. That means that the law is not allowed and cannot be enforced by the government.

For example, imagine that our government passed a law that said only persons born in The Bahamas are allowed to vote in elections. This law would be unconstitutional because Article 54 in our Constitution states that every **citizen** has the right to vote, regardless of where they were born.

### What is a citizen?

A citizen is a person who is recognised by law as a member of a country. When you are a citizen of a country, you have the right to live there, work there, and use the services and benefits that the country offers. But you also have responsibilities, like obeying the country's laws and paying taxes to support public services like schools and hospitals.

**Word power**

citizen

▲ A Bahamian citizen can get a Bahamian passport for international travel

**Connections**

# How do you become a citizen of The Bahamas?

**By birth**
If you were born
in The Bahamas and your
parents are citizens or
permanent residents,
you are automatically
a citizen

**By descent**
If you were born outside
The Bahamas and at least
one of your parents is a citizen,
you are automatically
a citizen

**By registration**
If you are married to a citizen or you have lived
in The Bahamas legally for a certain time, you
can apply to be
registered as
a citizen without
taking citizenship
tests

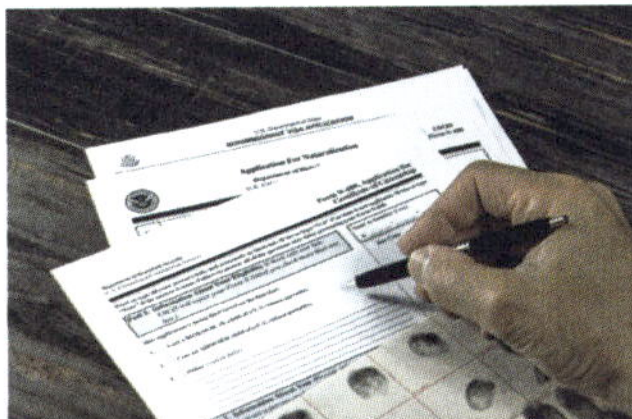

**By naturalisation**
If you have lived in The Bahamas for a certain
time and you meet other requirements, such as
passing a language
and citizenship test,
you can apply to
become a naturalised
citizen

## Activity 1 Discuss citizenship applications

1 A person who is not automatically a citizen must take two tests when applying to become a
citizen of The Bahamas:

   a The first test is a language test to show that the applicant can speak English well enough to
   live and work here. Why do you think the immigration services test this?

   b The second test checks whether the applicant knows important things about our history,
   government and national symbols. Write down five questions that would be good for this test.

   c Why do you think countries have citizenship tests like these?

2 A person applying for citizenship by naturalisation must publish a notice in the Government
Gazette and a local newspaper about their application. The notice must give their name,
address and current nationality, and a sentence like the one below:

'Any person who knows of any reason why this applicant should not be naturalised as a citizen
of The Bahamas is requested to communicate such reasons to the Minister of Immigration
within 21 days of the publication of this notice.'

   a Why do you think the government makes people do this?

   b List three reasons that people might give for why a person should not be allowed to become
   a citizen.

## Activity 2 Compare citizenship laws in different countries

1 The Bahamas does not allow citizens over the age of 21 to hold dual citizenship.

  **a** What is dual citizenship?

  **b** Find out if you can hold dual citizenship if you are a citizen of Switzerland, Australia, Brazil or Japan.

2 Copy this table and complete it to show how you can legally obtain citizenship in each country.

| Country | By birth | By descent | By registration | By naturalisation |
|---|---|---|---|---|
| The Bahamas | | | | |
| Brazil | | | | |
| Australia | | | | |
| Switzerland | | | | |
| Japan | | | | |
| South Africa | | | | |

## Changing the Constitution

Our Constitution came into law in 1973 when our country became independent. Since then, ideas and views about the world have changed. For example, the original Constitution did not give the same rights to men and women and the rights of persons with disabilities were not specifically protected.

The Constitution is a law. That means it can only be changed (amended) by an Act of Parliament. The Constitution describes the rules for changing any part of it. If the changes affect the rights and freedoms of Bahamians, the government must get approval from the citizens by holding a **referendum**. In a referendum, adult citizens answer yes or no to certain questions. At least 60% of the voters must answer yes for the proposal to be accepted.

**Word power**

referendum

## Activity 3 Summarise how laws are made

Work with a partner.

1 Write a short summary to outline the process that a bill goes through to become law. Use these words in your summary:

bill   first reading   debate   senate   house of assembly

third reading   vote   approved   signed   Act of Parliament

2 In 2021, the Constitution was changed by The Constitution (Amendment) (No.3) Act, 2021, which was passed by the Parliament of The Bahamas and came into force on May 6, 2021.

  **a** Discuss the process that would have allowed this Act of Parliament to be passed.

  **b** Find out how a referendum works. Draw a flowchart to explain the process.

## Law enforcement agencies

**Connections**



| The Royal Bahamas Police Force | The Royal Bahamas Defence Force | Correctional Services |
| --- | --- | --- |
| Headed by Commissioner | Headed by Commodore | Headed by Superintendent |
| Deals with crime and keeps peace and order on land | Deals with crime and keeps peace and order at sea | Manages prisons and keeps prisoners safe |

### Activity 4 Compare law enforcement agencies

1 Compare the badges of the three agencies. What does each agency's motto tell you about their work?

2 Which law enforcement agency would deal with these issues:

   **a** illegal fishing and removal of endangered species

   **b** election safety

   **c** offering training to help people get jobs when they leave prison

   **d** a break-in at a shop

   **e** working with the US Coastguard to prevent drug trafficking?

3 Members of law enforcement agencies wear uniforms.

   **a** Choose one law enforcement officer you see in your community. Draw the uniform they wear.

   **b** Why do you think members of law enforcement agencies wear uniforms? Give two reasons.

   **c** When might a law enforcement officer not wear a uniform? Why?

# Customs officers help to enforce the law

Customs officers work at airports and ports to make sure that things that come in and out of the country are safe and legal. They check things like people's passports, bags and packages to make sure they do not have anything illegal or dangerous inside.

Customs officers also make sure that businesses and individuals are following the rules for importing and exporting goods, and paying the correct import and export duties which helps the economy of The Bahamas.

▲ **A customs officer checking a passenger's bag at an airport**

### Activity 5 Draw a comic strip

Work in pairs. Imagine you are customs officers at the airport.

1 Discuss what things might go well during a shift at work.

2 Think about some things that might not go well. How would you deal with them?

3 Work together to draw a cartoon strip with speech bubbles showing one good experience and one bad experience during a customs officer's shift.

## Correctional services help to enforce the law

Prison officers must make sure that prisoners stick to the rules of the prison and that they cannot escape from prison. They also make sure that prisoners are safe and prepare them for moving back to society. For example, they try to prevent substance abuse and violence, they make sure prisoners get help for mental health problems and they offer training and education programmes.

### Activity 6 How can systems be improved?

Work in groups.

Both customs and prison officers often face challenges in their work.

1 Brainstorm a list of challenges that a prison officer might face.

2 What could be done to improve the work conditions and make the prison officer's job less challenging? Discuss your ideas.

**Reflection**

Which job do you think you are more suited for: customs officer or prisons officer? Why?

# The Ministry of Finance

**In this unit, you will:**

- define the terms ministry, finance, cabinet, banking, budget, and economy
- identify the Minister of Finance and outline the role of the Ministry of Finance
- discuss how the Ministry of Finance works with development banks and other ministries to address global issues that affect our economy and environment.

## What does the Ministry of Finance do?

The Ministry of Finance is responsible for overseeing and managing the government's resources and our country's finances.

The Minister of Finance is a member of the **cabinet** and meets with the government regularly to report on **finances**. One of the key roles of the finance minister is to present the national **budget**.

A budget is a financial plan that allows you to estimate how much money you will earn (revenue). It also gives details of how you will spend the money (expenditure).

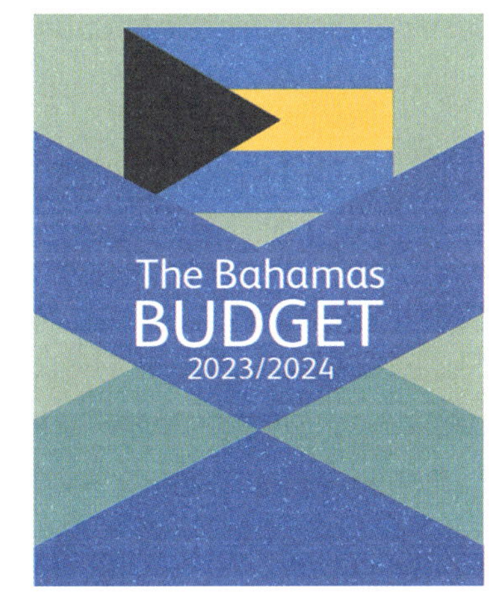



**Word power**

cabinet
finances
budget

A new budget is presented to parliament on the last Wednesday of May each year. The Minister of Finance gives a speech about the budget, providing detailed documents to show how much revenue the government hopes to earn and how this money will be spent. Members of Parliament get a chance to ask questions and debate the budget before it is approved (at the start of July).

### Activity 1 Find out about the Ministry of Finance

1  Who is the current Minister of Finance?
2  Where is the Ministry of Finance located?
3  The Ministry of Finance has a Treasury Department and an Economic Unit. What is the main role of each of these agencies?

**Tips**

You can ask people in your community about this and you can do research online to find out more about the Ministry of Finance.

Modern technical training centre

Skilled students

Better job opportunities and earning power

Economic growth

**Word power**

economy

**Example 1**

## Activity 2 Write an invitation letter

How would you invite someone from the Ministry of Finance to come and visit your school?

1 Work in a group to draft a formal letter of invitation. You will need to include:
   - suggested date and time
   - details of your school
   - three questions that your class would like answered.
2 Read out your letters to the class.
3 If possible, choose one letter and send it off to invite a guest speaker.

# Spending for economic growth and development

The government spends money to provide services and to help grow our **economy**. Economic growth means an increase in the goods and services produced in a country. This leads to more jobs and greater income for people. For example, an increase in tourism can lead to more jobs and more revenue for people and the government.

Examples of government spending include building roads, schools and hospitals, employing more teachers or police officers and funding agricultural projects to help communities grow more food. The government invests in areas such as education, infrastructure, and research and development, to encourage economic growth and support sustainable development.

The examples on this page and the next page show how a decision to spend money in one area can help to grow the economy and help our country develop in sustainable ways.

## Activity 3 Create an imaginary budget

Work in small groups. Imagine you are charge of drawing up the budget for a small island country.

Your budget is fixed. You have 100 units of money in total.

1 Make a list of the different sectors that must get a share of the budget, such as security services, health care and education.
2 Decide how you would share the 100 units of money between these sectors.
3 Draw a diagram to show how you divide up the budget.
4 Present your budget to the class.
5 Explain how you decided how to split the money between sectors.

## Activity 4 Show how investment leads to growth and development

**1** Consider these three investments. Draw a flowchart for each to show how it can contribute to the economy and development of our country.

**A**

Fund the creation of protected marine reserves

**B**

Train young people to keep bees and produce honey for sale.

**C**

Provide finance to businesses and homes to install solar energy systems.

**2** The Ministry of Finance published three aims for the national budget:

> Aim 1: Reduce the cost of living for all Bahamians.
>
> Aim 2: Provide opportunities for economic growth.
>
> Aim 3: Protect the security of our borders and resources.

**a** Discuss each aim. Say why it is important and how spending the country's money on this aim contributes to the economy and sustainable development.

**b** Give an example of one way that the government might spend money to achieve each of these aims.

## Countries borrow money to fund projects

When the government has to fund a very expensive project, they may borrow money (capital) to pay for it. For example, our government borrows money from **banks** such as the Inter-American Development Bank (IADB).

The IADB uses capital from member states and invests it to raise more money. When a member state takes a loan, they agree to pay it back with interest. The IADB also offers support to poorer countries in the form of grants. A grant does not have to be repaid.

**Example 2**

Investment in green energy projects

Reduce dependence on fossil fuels

Spend less on fuel imports

Promote sustainable development

**Word power**

bank

## Activity 5 Learn about the work of a development bank

The headquarters of the Inter-American Development Bank are in Washington DC. Visit the IADB website (www.iadb.org) and take a virtual tour of the bank.

Have a class discussion to share what you learnt during the virtual tour.

## Activity 6 Discuss the conditions for borrowing money

1 Would it be sensible to lend money to someone if you knew they would not be able to pay it back? Give reasons for your answers.

2 In 2023, our government took a loan from the IADB to fund a project to strengthen disaster risk management.

   a What do you think a country has to do before the IADB gives them a loan? Why?

   b The IADB also provides grants to the very poor member states. What is the difference between a loan and a grant?

   c What are the benefits of wealthier countries funding grants to help poorer countries to grow their economies?

   d Countries that take loans from the IADB have to pay the loan back over time with interest. How does this help the country and the bank?

## Activity 7 Sort economic activities

The Bahamas Development Bank funds projects that can help to grow our economy in three different areas:

- **The blue economy** is all the economic activities that generate wealth from the world's oceans and coasts.

- **The green economy** focuses on reducing pollution, clean energy sources energy and efficient use of resources to protect biodiversity and ecosystems.

- **The orange economy** focuses on creativity and included goods, services and activities linked to culture, creative arts, and heritage.

1 Draw a table with a column for each colour economy.

2 Sort these development areas into the different economies. Write them in the correct columns in your table.

- Renewable energy
- Tourism and cultural heritage
- Environmentally friendly buildings
- Performing arts
- Fisheries
- Waste management
- Music
- Sustainable transport
- Land management
- Mining and energy

### Reflection

Why is it very important for the Ministry of Finance to work closely with the Ministry of the Environment and Natural Resources? Give three reasons.

# 10 The United Nations

In this unit, you will:
- define the role of the United Nations
- discuss how political leaders work with the United Nations to achieve global goals
- identify some concerns of the United Nations
- create a model UN in your school.

## The role of the United Nations

The United Nations (UN) is the largest international organisation in the world. In 2023 the UN had 193 member countries. The Vatican (Holy See) and the State of Palestine are not members of the UN, but they have special status as permanent observers. Member countries pay membership fees to belong to the UN. The money collected from members is used to fund the work of the UN and its agencies.

▲ A banner from the UN website. You can see the symbol used by the UN. The slogan tells you about the aims of the UN

The UN has 4 main aims:
- Maintain international peace and security.
- Develop friendly relations between countries.
- Work towards solving international economic, social and cultural problems.
- Promote respect for human rights and freedom.

### Activity 1 Prepare a talk on the role of the UN

Imagine you are a government official. You have been asked to talk to a group of school children to explain to them why it is important to be a member of the UN and how being a member benefits your country and other members.

1 What would you say in your speech?
2 Write short notes of the key points you would make.
3 Practise your speech and then present it to the class.

# UN Agencies and their roles



The UN contains several smaller groups, called **agencies**, that deal with specific issues.

This table gives the names of five important UN agencies and describes their work.

| Agency | Focus area |
| --- | --- |
| Food and Agricultural Organization (FAO) | The main agency for rural development. Works to reduce poverty and hunger by promoting agriculture and improved food security, and tries to promote healthy nutrition |
| World Food Programme (WFP) | Provides food in the event of a natural disaster or other emergency |
| World Health Organization (WHO) | Works in all areas of health to prevent disease and educate people about health issues Collects data and provides support during pandemics |
| United Nations Development Programme (UNDP) | Works to eliminate poverty, restore and protect the environment, create employment opportunities, and advance the position of women in societies |
| United Nations Children's Fund (UNICEF) | Works to protect children worldwide and supports programmes that aim to improve children's lives |

**Connections**

## Activity 2 Research the work of UN agencies

1 Choose one of the agencies in the table. Visit their website and find out about their recent work. Make a poster about this.

2 Find out what UNESCO, UNCTAD and UNEP stand for. What is the focus area of each of these agencies?

3 Each UN agency has its own logo. What do you think the logos of UNICEF and the World Food Programme look like? Why? Use the internet to check if you were correct.

# The work of the UN and its agencies to achieve global goals

The UN works with political leaders from different countries to achieve global aims.

## Peacekeeping

The United Nations Emergency Force (UNEF) works to keep order and peace in regions where there is conflict, where it seems likely that there will be conflict or where there is a need for emergency aid (such as after an earthquake or hurricane). Political leaders from different countries send volunteers from their military forces to act as peacekeepers. The soldiers wear their own uniforms, but they all wear a light blue UN helmet so everyone recognises them as peacekeepers. The Bahamas has contributed to UN peacekeeping forces in several countries, including Haiti.

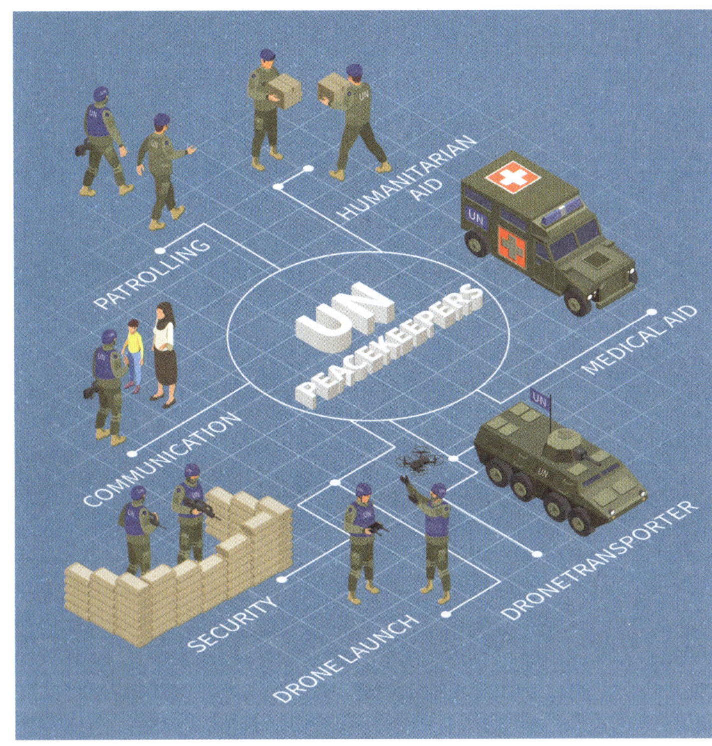


▲ Functions of UN peacekeepers

## Climate change

You already know that **climate change** is a global issue. One of the aims of the UN is to get countries to reduce the amount of carbon they release into the atmosphere. Political leaders work with the UN in different ways to meet these aims. For example:

- Leaders may join international agreements, such as the Paris Agreement that aims to limit global warming.
- Politicians can take part in UN Climate Conferences to meet other leaders and work together to take climate action.
- Governments can contribute to the Green Climate Fund to help poorer nations move towards cleaner energy supplies.
- Politicians can raise awareness of the issues locally and encourage their neighbouring states to join them in acting on climate change.

**Activity 3** Discuss the work of the UN after Hurricane Dorian

After Hurricane Dorian hit The Bahamas, the UNDP, UNICEF and WHO all sent assistance to the region.

What do you think each of these agencies helped with?

## Activity 4 Create a model UN at school

The structure of the UN is similar to the structure of a government. Look at the diagram below.

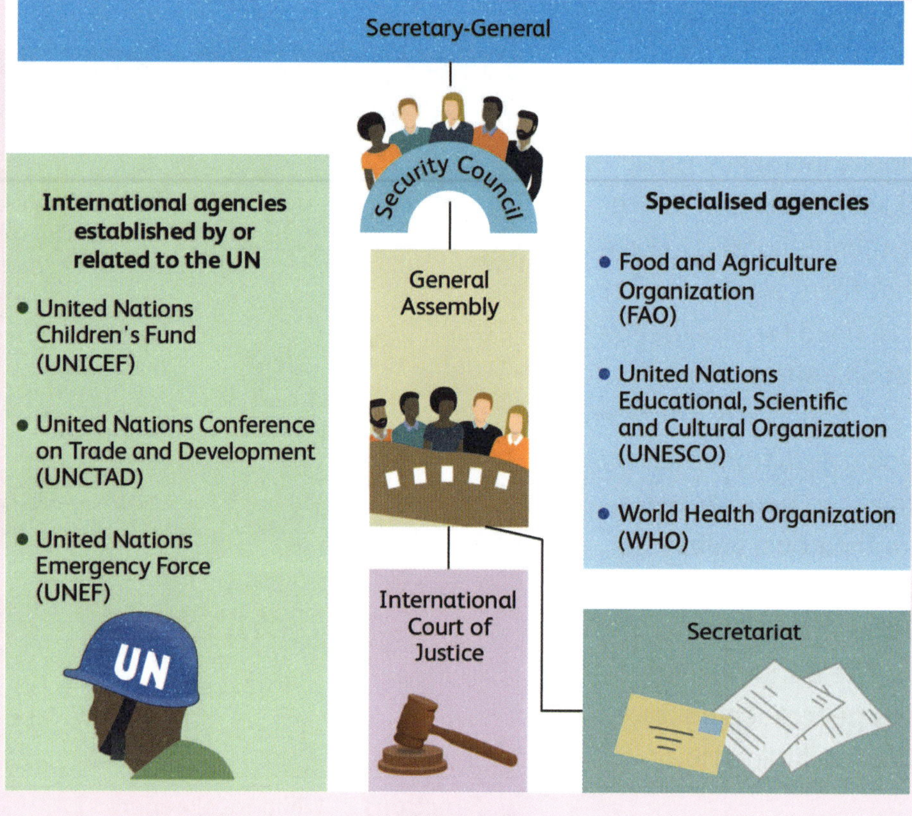


> **Reflection**
>
> Imagine you get a chance to spend time observing the work of one of the UN agencies. Which agency would you choose? Why?

1  Discuss the structure of the UN.

   **a**  How is it similar to the structure of a government?

   **b**  How is it different?

2  Work as a class to create an organisation like the UN for your school. Decide on the following:

   • What will you call your organisation?

   • Who will head up the organisation?

   • Where will the administration be done?

   • How many members will there be in the General Assembly?

   • How will decisions be made?

   • What will happen if members do not stick to the rules of the organisation?

   • What smaller groups or agencies will there be to help do the work of the organisation?

3  Make a large poster for the class to show the structure of your school organisation.

# 11 The world of work

**In this unit, you will:**

- define the terms human resources and civil servants
- explain how managing human resources well can contribute to quality of life
- give examples of how poorly managed human resources can affect a country
- distinguish between the government and private sector in The Bahamas
- evaluate the effects of migrating to work in different parts of the country
- examine how workers move between countries and analyse the positive and negative impacts of employing foreign workers.

## Human resources

You already know that natural resources are the things found in nature and used by people. Beautiful beaches, water, fish, coconuts, conch and aragonite are all natural resources.

People who use their ideas and work to provide services or make goods are called **human resources**. Teachers, tour guides, mechanics and chocolate makers are all examples of human resources.

### Managing human resources

Managing human resources well and protecting workers' rights can help to improve the quality of life for everyone in a country.

Here are some ways for a country to manage human resources well:

- Invest in education and training to help create more job opportunities.
- Develop a skilled and well-trained workforce to encourage businesses to invest here.
- Provide good healthcare for all citizens to provide jobs in this sector and to help people lead productive lives.
- Encourage creativity and entrepreneurship as this can lead to new industries and job opportunities.
- Pass laws that protect workers and make sure that they are paid fairly and treated with respect.

**Word power**

human resources

▲ The Bahamas is rich in natural resources

▲ Human resources are the people who provide services or make goods

## Activity 1 Make a poster

Work in groups to plan and make a poster to show why it is important for government and other employers to care for the people that do the work in a country.

1 Think of a catchy slogan, for example:

> **It pays to care for people**

> **People are our most valuable resource**

2 Give at least two examples of good human resource management and show how each helps the economy and makes people's lives better.
3 Add pictures and labels to make your poster attractive.
4 Display your completed poster in the classroom.

## What happens when human resources are not well managed?

When a country does not manage its human resources very well, it can cause problems for the country, the economy and the people who live there.

## Activity 2 Cause and effect

Below are some examples of poor human resource management. For each example, write down what effect it might have on the country and the people who live there.

> A   People are not trained or educated well.

> B   Poor opportunities mean that skilled workers leave to work in other countries.

> C   There are not enough nurses or doctors.

> D   The schools are poorly equipped and teachers are not properly trained.

> E   Workers' rights are not protected by the labour laws.

# Sharing resources

When countries work together and help each other, they can make sure that people are taken care of and have a good quality of life.

There are different ways that countries can work together to manage human resources and help each other get the resources they need.

Countries can:

- share knowledge and learn from each other how to manage resources well
- help each other by giving money (through development banks or other agencies) and lending resources to complete projects (such as engineers to build roads or experts to train teachers).
- hire skilled foreign workers to fill gaps in their own country
- take part in exchange programmes, such as student or teacher exchange where people visit each other's countries to learn from them
- sign agreements that protect workers' rights and set out conditions of employment, for example in CARICOM or other organisations.

## Reflection

1. If you could take part in a student exchange programme, which country would you like to go to? Why?

2. What do you think you could learn by taking part in an exchange programme? How would this help you and your community?

3. If you could invite students from three different countries to be part of an exchange programme at your school, which countries would you choose? Why?

# The public and private sectors

In our country, like many others, the labour system can be divided into two parts: the public or government sector and the private sector.

People who work in the public sector are employed by the government, government agencies or government-owned businesses. All public officials and **civil servants** are employed by the government.

People who work in the private sector are employed by privately owned individual businesses.

Tourism is the largest source of employment in The Bahamas. Almost 50% of all people work directly in tourism, and many more work indirectly in tourism support services. Both the public and private sectors are involved in the tourist industry.

> **Word power**
>
> civil servant

▲ **Tourism is the largest source of employment in The Bahamas**

## Activity 3 Sort businesses into sectors

Work in groups.

1 Discuss all the people that a tourist will deal with as they book their trip, travel to The Bahamas, arrive here, spend time here and then leave.

  a Make a list of as many jobs as you can that are linked to travel and tourism in The Bahamas.

  b Study your list. Which jobs are in the private sector? Which are in the public sector?

2 Consider the jobs below. For each one, say whether the person is employed in the public or private sector.

- Conservation officer in marine reserve
- Customs officer
- Minister of Tourism
- Hotel cleaner
- Guest house owner
- Food stall owner
- Market stall holder
- Tour guide
- Snorkelling instructor
- Tourist police
- Cruise ship beautician

## Moving for work

When people cannot find a job where they live, they may decide to migrate (move) elsewhere to look for work. People may also migrate to find better opportunities, nicer living conditions, higher wages and a different lifestyle.

In The Bahamas, people who work in tourism and construction often move between islands for work.

▲ Natural disasters can cause people to migrate. After Hurricane Dorian destroyed infrastructure in 2019, people who worked in tourism were left without jobs. The tourist authorities set up a special appeal to find jobs on other islands so people could support themselves and their families

**Activity 4** Discuss the effects of moving between islands for work

Work in groups. Discuss each question.

1  What are some of the advantages of migrating from smaller to larger islands in search of work?
2  What problems might a person have if they move from a village to a larger town or city to look for work?
3  How can migration negatively affect smaller islands?
4  Why do you think people who work in tourism or construction are most likely to migrate for work?

## Migrating between countries

Read what different people are saying about migrating to another country to work there.

## Activity 5 Identify positive and negative impacts of foreign workers

1 How do foreign workers like Tia, Matt, Kev, Otto and Sakura contribute positively to The Bahamas? Think about:

- skills and knowledge

- filling gaps in certain fields

- contributing to economic growth and development

- creating global connections

2 Can you think of any negative effects of having foreign workers in a country? Share your ideas with your group.

3 Bahamians also take jobs outside the country. For example, many Bahamians migrate to other countries to work in healthcare, finance and tourism. Young people who study in another country may stay on to work there. When a country loses skilled and experienced workers, it is called a brain drain.

   a Discuss what the term 'brain drain' means.

   b What do you think a 'brain gain' is?

   c Think of two reasons why a country might have a brain drain.

### Reflection

Should anyone who wants to be free to migrate to and from The Bahamas for work? Give reasons for your answer.

# 12 Manufacturing



## What is manufacturing?

**Word power**

manufacturing

**Manufacturing** means making goods. Manufacturing is also called industry. Factories use machinery and other equipment to process resources and make finished products. For example, a factory might use cotton fabric and screen-printing machinery to manufacture T-shirts and print them with the logo of a cruise line.

There are two types of manufacturing:

- Heavy industry uses big, heavy machines to make very large products or metal goods in large factories. Shipbuilding is an example of a heavy industry.

- Light industry uses small, light machines to make smaller items. The machines may be in a factory or someone's home. Canning food is an example of a light industry.

### Activity 1 Classify manufacturing industries

**1** How would you classify each of these manufacturing industries? Give reasons for your decisions.

▲ Making clothes

▲ Making cement

▲ Making cars

▲ Making paper towels

▲ Shipbuilding

▲ Making chocolate

**2** Write down another example of a heavy industry and a light industry.

# Local manufacturing industries

Manufacturing industries play a fairly small part in our economy. In 2021, manufacturing contributed just over 11% to the economy, while tourism and financial services contributed almost 80%.

Some major industries in The Bahamas are cement manufacturing, breweries, pharmaceutical (medicines) plants, spiral-welded steel pipe manufacturing, chocolate factories, and paper processing to make toilet paper, tissues and paper towels.

The largest industrial park and manufacturing area in The Bahamas is found at Freeport, on Grand Bahama.

When a country does not make the goods they need, they must import them. Imported goods often cost more than locally made ones because they are made elsewhere and transported to The Bahamas to be sold.

The Government and The Bahamas Development Bank are working to encourage more local manufacturing to create jobs and reduce the amount of goods we import. Reducing imports will save the country money.

This flowchart shows how developing local manufacturing industries can benefit the country:

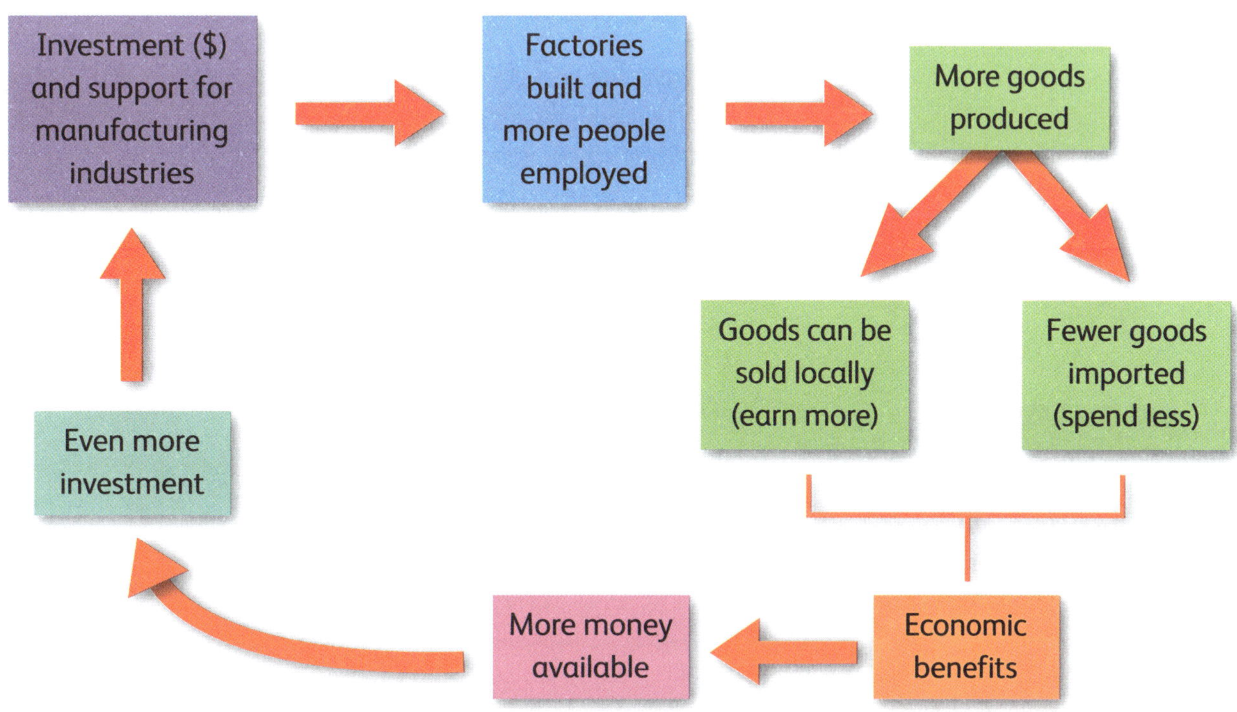

The case study below is an example of how the government and the Bahamas Development Bank support the development of local manufacturing industries.

## Case study

### Manufacturing coconut oil and other products

The Bahamas Development Bank (BDB) would like to support local industry by investing in projects to manufacture coconut oil and coconut oil-based hair products locally. Currently, coconut oil is imported from The Philippines.

Projects would be able to use local natural resources – coconuts – which grow easily in The Bahamas. Small factories can produce value-added products (such as coconut oil). The BDB offers funding for working capital (buying supplies, paying salaries and marketing) and equipment. It will also offer technical support to increase production on all islands and provide training courses and opportunities.

## Activity 2 Developing local manufacturing

Read the case study. Discuss these questions in your group:

1  How would this project help develop local industry?
2  What benefits would there be if The Bahamas did not need to import coconut oil?
3  What will the BDB do to help grow this industry? Why are these things important?

## Activity 3 Research local industrial areas

1  Discuss these questions in your group:
   a  Why do you think factories are often grouped together in one area?
   b  What are the benefits of having an industrial park near the port and other transport routes?
2  Where are the main industrial areas on your island? Draw a sketch map and label it to show what industries are found there.
3  a  If you could develop two manufacturing industries on your island, what would they be? Give reasons for your choices.
   b  Explain where you would locate each industry.
   c  Explain how it would benefit the local economy and contribute to developing our country.

## Reflection

What was the most interesting thing you learned in this unit? What made it interesting to you?

# 13 Communication and transport

**In this unit, you will:**

- define the terms communication and transport
- identify how packages and documents move around the world
- summarise how transport is used to import and export goods
- draw conclusions about the links between transport and communication.

## Modern communications

**Communication** means sharing information, news and ideas.

Communication can be face-to-face, such as when your teacher communicates with you in class or when you talk to your friends.

Communication can also happen at a distance: when you send a text message or email, you are communicating at a distance.

Modern technology has made it very easy for people to communicate at a distance and to share information with other people in different parts of the world almost instantly.

> **Word power**
>
> communication

### Activity 1 Different forms of communication

1  Which of these means of communication do you use? List them in order from the one you use most to the one you use least.

 Television

 Mobile phone

 Newspapers

 Radio

Landline

 Magazines

 Letters/cards

 Internet

 Mobile calls

 Emails

2  Draw a labelled diagram to show how modern communication systems allow you to communicate instantly with a friend who lives in Australia.

# Transporting goods and documents



**Transportation** involves moving goods, documents or people from place to place, using different means of transport.

Efficient transport systems are important for economic growth and development. In The Bahamas, tourism relies on air and sea transport to bring tourists to the country, as well as local road and ferry services to let tourists move around when they are in the country. Trade relies on importing and exporting goods by air or ship. Containers of goods are shipped through Freeport and Prince George. Locally, people need transport to get to work and school, and people, post and goods need to be transported to islands.

The Department of Customs and Immigration is responsible for controlling the movement of goods and people into and out of the country. Customs officers at airports and ports check that people entering or leaving The Bahamas have the correct travel documents and that they are not bringing dangerous or illegal goods into the country.

Customs officers also inspect goods that are imported and exported through our ports. They may open shipping containers to make sure they contain the goods that are listed on import/export forms. They may also open parcels sent to individuals or businesses and charge a fee (import duties) that must be paid before the parcel can be collected.

Mailboats are The Bahamas' largest domestic shipping distribution network, delivering time-sensitive cargo (and sometimes people) to every rock, cay and/or island in The Bahamas.

▲ **A mail boat about to leave Nassau**

## Activity 2 Transporting mail and small packages

Post and small packages are delivered to the main post office in Nassau every day.

1. How do you think post and small packages are transported to The Bahamas?
2. When you receive a package you may have to pay import duties and VAT. Which government departments decide these rates?
3. Mr Samuels lives in Eleuthera. He orders a package from a large online store. The store only delivers to Nassau. How do you think it gets from Nassau to his home?
4. Why is a mailboat service important in our country? Give three reasons.

# Modern technology, transport and communication

Modern technology allows us to use communication systems to transport documents, money and media electronically. Read these examples.

**Zara** needs to renew her passport. She fills in the renewal form on the government website. She takes a photo using her phone and uploads it to the computer. Then she enters her credit card details to pay the renewal fee. She checks the details and then presses 'send' to submit her application instantly.

**Jerry** loves to read. He used to order books and have them posted to his house. Now he goes online, orders the books he wants and pays for them electronically. The books are delivered instantly to his computer and he reads them on-screen.

**Keshia** orders a new credit card. While she is waiting for the plastic card to arrive in the post, she can use an electronic card on the banking app on her smartphone.

**Rayshawn** loves music and movies. He used to buy CDs and rent movies to watch at home. Now he pays a monthly fee (which is taken automatically from his bank account) and downloads the music and movies he wants.

**A school library** subscribes to a geographical magazine. The magazine used to be shipped from the USA to Nassau and then it was transported to the school on the mail boat. The magazine would arrive about three weeks after it was published. This year, the school took an electronic subscription. The magazine is delivered instantly to the school library and students can read it on a computer.

Technology also allows import and export businesses to track goods. Companies can track the exact position of a ship using global positioning satellites and customers can log in to websites to find out where their parcels are at any time and when they will be delivered.

## Activity 3 Find out about satellite communications

Work in pairs.
1 Use the internet or library resources to find out how the global positioning system (GPS) works with satellites in space to track a ship on Earth.
2 Draw a simple labelled diagram. Show the main parts of the system and what each part does.

**Reflection**

How can you make sure you are safe when you are using the internet? Share your ideas with your group.

## Theme 2  What have you learnt?

### Unit 8 Citizenship and the Constitution

**1** Match the definitions on the left to the correct terms on the right.

> **a** the highest law of a country
>
> **b** questions to see if you can speak English and know about the country where you are settling
>
> **c** process of getting citizenship by fulfilling some conditions and doing a test
>
> **d** travel document that citizens can apply for to leave the country
>
> **e** citizenship of more than one country at the same time

> dual citizenship
> naturalisation
> passport
> Constitution
> citizenship test

**2** Milly was born on Cat Island while her parents were on holiday. Both her parents are Brazilian citizens. Is Milly a Bahamian citizen by birth? Explain why you think so.

**3** Rayshawn was born in Geneva in Switzerland. His dad is a Bahamian citizen who works for the UN. His mom is Swiss. Explain why Rayshawn qualifies to be a Bahamian citizen.

### Unit 9 The Ministry of Finance

**4** Who is the Minister of Finance?

**5** Explain in your own words what a budget is.

**6** Complete this flowchart to show the process that the annual budget goes through before it is signed into law.

### Unit 10 The United Nations

**7** Decide whether each statement is true or false. If it is false, correct it.

  **a** The UN headquarters are in London.

  **b** The King of England is the head of the UN.

  **c** The Secretariat takes care of the administration of the UN.

  **d** The UN has its own army.

  **e** The UN promotes peace, democracy and human rights.

**8** Choose one agency of the UN. Write the name of the agency and the main focus of its work.

**(Continued)**

## Unit 11 The world of work

**9** Explain the difference between human and natural resources.

**10** Draw a diagram to show how the labour system in The Bahamas is structured.

**11** How can moving from one island to another for work affect both islands?

**12** List two positive and two negative effects of employing foreign workers in The Bahamas.

## Unit 12 Manufacturing

**13** Use information from this diagram to write a paragraph explaining the benefits of developing local manufacturing industries for the community and country.

| Local manufacturing | Investing in people | Skills creation | Grow local economies | Job creation |

**14** Graycliff Chocolate Factory and The Bahamas Rum Cake Factory are both located in Nassau. Describe what each factory manufactures, what equipment they need and whether they are light or heavy industries.

**15** Name three heavy industries found in the industrial park at Freeport.

## Unit 13 Communication and transport

**16** Write an email to a friend who was absent and missed the lesson about transporting goods and documents. Explain how people can send a package or letter to another island, how goods are imported into our country and how modern technology can be used to send documents and money electronically to other places in the world.

**17** Imagine you are a small farmer in Bimini. What would be the best way for you to send each of these to Nassau? Give a reason for your choice.

   **a** fresh coconuts    **b** your family    **c** wedding invitations.

# 14 Learning about the past



## What is history?

**Word power**

history
source
timeline
era

**History** tells us about events and people from the past. Historians use different **sources** of information to build up a picture of what happened in the past. Sources can be written materials, such as diaries and letters, or they can be physical remains, such as buildings and other artefacts.

A **timeline** is a useful diagram for showing the order of events in the past, with dates and information about major events.

The history of The Bahamas before independence can be roughly divided into three **eras**, as shown in this timeline.

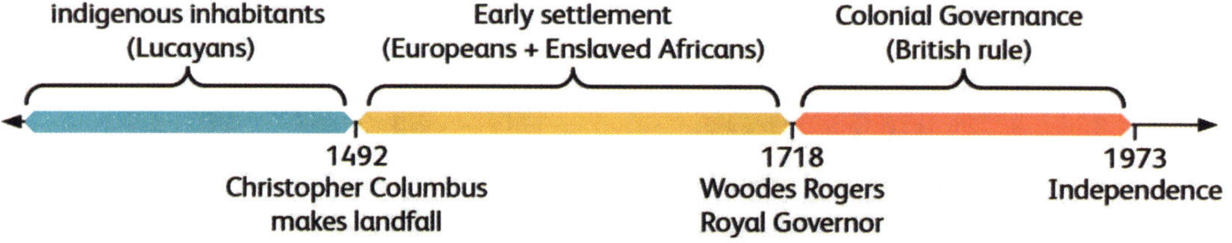


▲ Timeline of key events in the history of The Bahamas

### Activity 1 Create your own timeline

Draw a timeline to represent the period from 1492 (arrival of Columbus) to 1838 (emancipation of enslaved people).

- Add key events from this period of our history. You can use symbols and drawings to show events.
- Include information about:

the Eleutheran Adventurers  Pirates  Loyalists  Enslaved people

Woodes Rodgers  The Emancipation Act

# Ideas can change the world

When we study historical events, we can often understand what happened by considering the ideas or beliefs of the people involved. For example, Christopher Columbus believed that the world was round, not flat. This led him to leave Spain and sail westward in 1492. One of the first places he encountered was San Salvador (Guanahani) in The Bahamas. His voyages led in turn to colonisation and the birth of new nations.

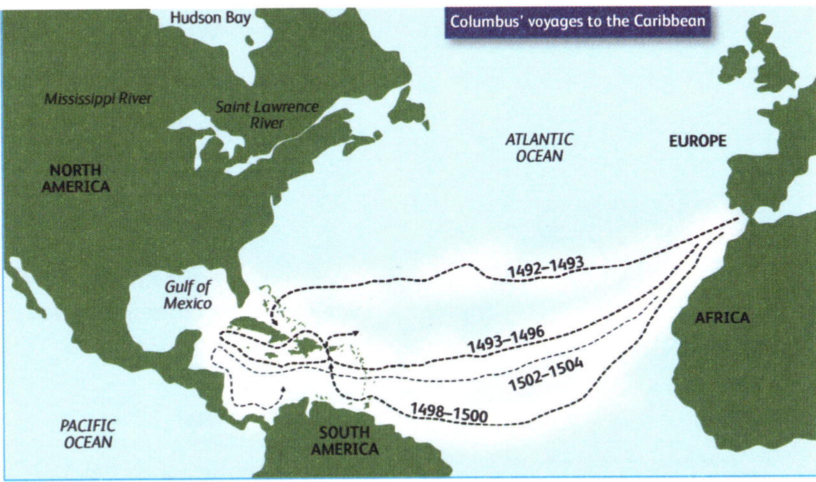


▲ **Christopher Columbus made several voyages. The map shows the routes he took on four different voyages. Use your atlas to work out which islands he encountered on each route.**

Christopher Columbus believed he had sailed around the world and reached India. For this reason, he called the islands he encountered 'The West Indies'. Once he returned to Europe and told people about his discoveries, more people from Europe came to our region. The European settlers at that time believed they had the right to occupy the land and they disregarded or enslaved the original Lucayan settlers.

Christopher Columbus kept a journal. Read these two diary extracts from his diary from October 1492 before you do Activity 2:

*It appears to me, that the people are ingenious, and would be good servants and I am of opinion that they would very readily become Christians, as they appear to have no religion. They very quickly learn such words as are spoken to them. If it please our Lord, I intend at my return to carry home six of them to your Highnesses, that they may learn our language.*

*'They came to the ship in canoes, made of a single trunk of a tree, wrought in a wonderful manner considering the country; some of them large enough to contain forty or forty-five men, others of different sizes down to those fitted to hold but a single person.'*

## Activity 2 Read a primary source

What do the extracts above tell you about:
1 Columbus and his views
2 the Lucayans?

# Learning about historical events

Journalists are taught to include answers to six key questions, called the Journalistic Six, in their articles: who, what, where, when, why and how. This helps them to make sure that they have covered the whole story.

**Who?**
- People involved
- Names or groups

**What?**
Describe the event. What happened?

**Where?**
Location where it happened, where people came from/went

**When?**
Try to give exact dates or period of time

**Why?**
Purpose of the event, what caused this to happen?

**How?**
How did the event begin/end, how did it affect people/places?

▲ The Journalistic Six questions

When you try to understand and learn about events in history, it is useful to think like a journalist and ask these questions about the event. Once you have asked and answered these questions, you can put all the information together to get a full picture of the event.

Captain William Sayle was the leader of a group called the Eleutheran Adventurers. Read this historical source about his group.

> It is 1647 and King Charles I of England, who rules Bermuda, wants us to join his church and become Protestants. We are in disagreement and want the freedom to worship in our own churches. It seems we will be forced to leave Bermuda and set sail to find a new settlement where there will be freedom and equal justice for all. Our new community will be known as Eleutheria, from the Greek word for freedom. We have set up a group called the Eleutheran Adventurers. All members of the group will pay £100 for the voyage and a parcel of land when we arrive. We hope to set sail next year.

## Activity 3 Write a factual paragraph

Apply the Journalistic Six questions to help you write a factual paragraph about the arrival of the Eleutheran Adventurers in The Bahamas. You may need to do some further research.

# Different groups of settlers

Different groups of people arrived and settled in The Bahamas at different times in our history. Each group brought with them new ideas and practices that led to changes in the way of life in our region and the development of new places and societies. If any of these groups of people had not settled here, our history would be very different.

## The Eleutheran Adventurers

The Eleutheran Adventurers sailed to The Bahamas in 1648 in two ships. Before they landed, one of the ships struck a reef. All their supplies, including food, were lost. They landed on the island of Eleuthera and established a settlement called Governor's Harbour. According to the history website, www.bahamianology.com, the Eleutherans brought 28 enslaved black persons with them.

▲ Eleutheran settlers at Governor's Harbour clearing land

The new settlers found life very difficult because they had lost most of their supplies in the shipwreck. Therefore, they decided to take their remaining ship and sail north to Virginia to ask for help. The community there gave them another ship and supplies to take back to Eleuthera. This event was the first of many links between The Bahamas and the USA.

Over time, the Eleutheran community grew and eventually moved to the island we now call New Providence.

## Activity 4 Eleutheran impact on our society

1  Discuss how the Eleutheran Adventurers contributed to our history. Consider:

religious freedom

trade routes with the USA

surnames

2  Today, people still come to The Bahamas to live here. Compare modern settlers with the Eleutheran Adventurers. Are they similar in any way? How are they different?

## The Age of Piracy

In the 1700s, there were many pirates in the Caribbean. Pirates made a living by capturing and robbing ships.

We asked an artificial intelligence (AI) programme to write us a short report about pirates and their impact on The Bahamas. This is the report it generated:

### Pirates and their impact on The Bahamas

During the 1700s, The Bahamas experienced a thrilling era known as the Age of Piracy. This was a time when daring pirates ruled the seas and made the islands their home. Famous pirates like Blackbeard, Calico Jack, and Black Bart roamed the Bahamian waters, seeking adventure and treasure. Not to be outdone, strong and fearless women pirates like Anne Bonny and Mary Read also made their mark in history.

The presence of these swashbuckling pirates had a significant impact on the settlements and society of The Bahamas. Some pirates used the islands as hiding spots to repair their ships and restock their supplies. This brought wealth and trade to the local communities. However, it also brought danger, as pirates sometimes raided these settlements, causing fear and disruption.

Life in the Bahamian settlements became a delicate balance between survival and lawlessness. People had to be cautious and ready to defend themselves. Some towns even built forts to protect against pirate attacks, and the locals formed militias to guard their homes and loved ones.

The pirates' presence also led to the rise of privateers, who were pirates sanctioned by governments to attack enemy ships. These privateers added another layer of excitement and danger to the islands.

Despite the chaos, the Age of Piracy left a legacy on The Bahamas. It shaped the culture and folklore of the islands, with tales of daring escapes and hidden treasure becoming part of local legends. The pirates' influence is still felt today through the names of certain places and the vibrant pirate festivals celebrated on the islands.

**Tips**

Read texts generated by AI critically. Think about what you already know and look out for things that might not be accurate.

## Activity 5 Evidence of the Age of Piracy

1. The photo shows the Pirates of Nassau Museum. What would you expect to see if you visited this museum? Why?

2. How did pirates affect our society and contribute to our history? Consider both positive and negative effects. Give examples and evidence to support your answer.

3. Do you think that an article written by AI will always be accurate? Discuss why or why not.

## The British take control

The British government wanted to put an end to piracy and bring law and order to the islands. They chose Woodes Rodgers to lead this mission. Woodes Rodgers arrived in The Bahamas in 1718. He brought a group of soldiers and sailors with him to help him in his task. He wanted to make the islands safe and secure for everyone. He offered a pardon to the pirates who were willing to give up their life of crime. Around 300 pirates accepted this offer, but others refused and were captured and put into prison.

Woodes Rodgers set up the first parliament and the British started to establish laws and maintain order. From 1718, The Bahamas was known as a British Crown Colony.

▶ **The seal of The Bahamas when it was a British Crown Colony**



### Activity 6 Write a diary entry

Imagine you were living in The Bahamas in 1718 when Woodes Rodgers arrived here. Write a diary entry describing your life at that time, and how the arrival of Woodes Rodgers changed that.

## The Loyalists

When America became independent of Britain, there were many people who did not want to be American. One group, called the Loyalists, decided to leave America and move to The Bahamas so they could continue to live under British rule.

When the Loyalists moved to The Bahamas in 1783, they brought their slaves with them. The population of the islands rose from 4,000 to 11,300. Many of the Loyalists were farmers. They moved to the family islands and set up cotton plantations. Others were fishermen who settled in Abaco and Eleuthera.

The Loyalists built many churches, including Christ Church Cathedral, and established schools. They started *The Gazette*, the first newspaper in The Bahamas. They also set up a police force and built a prison.

The Loyalists needed to trade and transport goods between the islands and the USA, so they improved docks and wharves, built a covered market in Nassau and made sure streets were well maintained.

**Connections**

Many of our buildings and ruins date back to the Loyalist period.

▲ **Christ Church Cathedral and the historic Balcony House in Nassau are good examples of Loyalist architecture**



### Activity 7 The impact of the Loyalists on our society

Work with a partner. Imagine you are both journalists who write articles for a history website. Work together to write a short article describing how the arrival of the Loyalists contributed to building the Bahamian society we have today.

## Enslaved Africans

The trans-Atlantic slave trade brought many enslaved Africans to the Caribbean. The Loyalists brought more enslaved Africans from America to The Bahamas to work on their plantations. Some freed slaves from America also settled in The Bahamas.

Today, 85% of our population have African heritage. The communities of Adelaide, Fox Hill and Bain's Town were established by enslaved Africans.

Enslaved Africans made a significant contribution to building The Bahamas. Their forced labour played a crucial role in building infrastructure, clearing land, cultivating crops and supporting the economy. Their skills, knowledge, and resilience shaped the development of the islands, yet they endured unimaginable hardships and injustices under the system of slavery. We cannot really understand our history and culture without recognising the massive contributions they made.



### Activity 8 Do a group project

Work in groups.

1 Make a poster showing how the slave trade and Junkanoo are linked and closely connected.

2 Write a short essay discussing the impact that the slave trade had on our society in the past and how that is reflected in our culture and way of life today.

# 15 Bahamian history prior to independence

**In this unit, you will:**
- explain the term 'The Contract' and discuss and analyse the effects it had on family life and the economy of The Bahamas
- discuss the events that led to majority rule, explaining why these happened and how they were resolved
- identify the role played by Sir Randol Fawkes in the labour movement
- discuss majority rule and analyse the concerns that led to majority rule
- sequence events that led to the independence of The Bahamas
- name political heroes that played a role in the independence movement and list their contributions
- analyse the events leading to independence and understand their significance.

## Migrating to work

In the 1940s, many people in The Bahamas were struggling to find ways to make a living:

- Improved sailing charts and maps and new lighthouses that warned ships of danger meant that the wrecking business was no longer profitable.
- Hurricanes in the 1930s damaged reefs and destroyed sponge beds.
- Although tourism was beginning to grow in the early 1900s, the start of the Second World War in 1939 meant that few tourists visited the islands.

During the war, many Americans joined up and were sent to Europe to fight with the countries that were allies of the USA. Farms and factories in the USA found it difficult to find workers.

The governments of the USA and The Bahamas agreed that Bahamian workers could get seasonal contracts to work in the USA. This became known as '**The Contract**' because each worker signed a contract agreeing to the terms of employment.

Between 1943 and 1947, 15,200 Bahamian men and women signed contracts and travelled to the USA to work. Most of the work was on farms, picking fruit and vegetables. Each worker was entitled to a set amount of money for their work.

▲ Many people in the sponging industry, like this woman shearing a sponge, could no longer make a living from sponging in The Bahamas

**Word power**

The Contract

The payments were divided into three parts: one part was paid to workers as wages, one part was placed into a savings fund and the third part was paid to the workers' families in The Bahamas. At the end of the contract, the money in the savings fund was paid out to the workers.

Read the extracts below about The Contract before doing Activity 1:

When The Contract started, nearly every Bahamian of every class, colour and educational status signed up to go. It was real money they were after, as The Bahamas was in a severe depression following the end of prohibition and the collapse of the sponge industry.

It wasn't uncommon for a hard-working person to come home after a four- or five-years' experience with three or four thousand dollars in the Post Office Bank. In the early 1950s and 60s, that was a lot of money to have in one place.

Economically and socially the migration of so many Bahamians to the United States to work on a temporary basis reshaped the community. Financially, many of the migrants benefitted from taking part in the programme. While each worker received a portion of his or her earned wages, another portion was placed in a savings fund, and yet another was sent home to family members. These savings enabled workers, the overwhelming majority of whom returned to The Bahamas, to finance homes, start businesses, and share money with family members who had remained in the islands. Socially, on the other hand, sometimes the programme disrupted family relations as a result of the absence of one or another spouse for extended periods of time. All told, "The Contract" would leave its mark on postwar Bahamian society for years to come.

In 1944, there were 5762 persons who went to work in the USA. At the time, that was around one-tenth of our population.

The immediate effect of The Contract was economic, real money. When you signed up to go if you were single, you could assign some of your earnings to a family member, but if single, it was compulsory to assign an amount to your mother.  If married, then naturally assignments were made to wives, but the system ensured that some of your earnings were remitted to The Bahamas.

Leaving home for the first time was exciting yet frightening. Some of us were exposed to one of the major problems facing America – racism.

## Activity 1 Work with sources

Work in pairs.

1   Read the extracts on the previous page. Discuss these questions:
    a   How did The Contract impact on family life? Why?
    b   Why did so many people choose to take up The Contract?
    c   What was the economic benefit for workers, their families and our country?
    d   One writer says The Contract left its mark on our society for years. What do you think that means?
2   a   Find one elderly person in your community. Ask politely if you can interview them to find out whether they remember being told what happened during The Contract and how it affected their family and community.
    b   Write a paragraph summarising what you found out.

# The road to majority rule 1942–1967

Think about a group of 10 friends trying to decide whether to watch a movie or go to the beach. The friends take a vote, and 7 of them choose the beach. This means that the majority (most of the friends) chose the beach. They all then follow that decision, even the three friends who voted for the movie.

In politics, **majority rule** means that the party that gets the most votes in a general election gets to govern the country. All citizens, even those who did not vote for the winning party, accept their right to govern.

▲ **A group of people voting about a decision they have to make**

Today, our country is governed by majority rule, but this was not always the case. Before the start of majority rule on 10 January 1967, decisions were mainly made by a few powerful individuals. Only people who owned land were allowed to vote. Majority rule changed that– it gave everyone the power to choose their own leaders and have a say in how the country was governed.

**Word power**

majority rule

Historians identify some key events that led to majority rule:

- Burma Road riot
- formation of political parties
- General Strike
- Women's Suffrage Movement
- Black Tuesday
- delegation to the United Nations.

## The Burma Road riot (1942)

Word power

Burma Road riot
The Project

The year 1942 was important in our country's history. An event known as the **Burma Road riot** raised awareness of workers' rights. It also highlighted the fact that people who did the same jobs should be paid the same, no matter what race, sex or nationality they were.

What was the Burma Road riot? In 1942, the British decided to build two military air bases in The Bahamas – one outside Nassau and the other in the west of New Providence. The construction of the air bases was known as **The Project**. It offered work for over 2000 local people.

At first, it seemed that everyone working on The Project would receive the same pay (8 shillings). Then the Bay Street Merchants (a powerful group of businessmen) convinced the contractors to pay local workers the usual rate of 4 shillings a day.

Workers felt this was not a fair wage and that they could not support themselves and their families on 4 shillings. When the workers found out they were being paid less than American workers who were doing the same jobs, they approached the newly formed Bahamas Federation of Labour with their complaints. The Labour Federation asked the government to increase the workers' wages. But many of the Bay Street Merchants were in the government and they denied the request.

Workers were angry. They downed tools and staged a protest march to Bay Street. On the way, many other people joined them and the protest, which lasted two days, turned into a riot with looting and some violence. The government eventually agreed to increase the rate of pay by one shilling per day (to 5 shillings) and to provide a free lunch. After five days, most of the workers returned to work.

## A new political era

These are some of the ideas people held after the Burma Road riots:

- Workers have the right to fair pay and decent conditions and they can organise and form groups to fight for and protect those rights.
- All citizens, rich and poor, should have the right to choose the leaders they want to represent them in government.
- The colonial government and Bay Street Merchants had too much power and they made decisions based on their own interests.

These ideas had a huge impact on our society and led to the establishment of political parties:

- The Progressive Liberal Party (PLP) was established to represent the ordinary citizens (mostly black) who were the majority of the population. The founding members were Henry Taylor, William Cartwright and Cyril Stevenson. Lyndon Pindling soon joined and became the party leader. The PLP aimed to gain a majority in the Assembly. Their goal was to represent all citizens – black and white – and move towards majority rule.
- The powerful members of the existing government were alarmed by the support for the PLP. They joined together to form the United Bahamian Party (UBP).
- Randol Fawkes and other labour organisers realised that it was important to represent the workers in government. They formed the much smaller Labour Party.
- The PLP gained votes and soon became the opposition party in Parliament. The Labour Party only had one seat (but it would be a very important seat in time).

▲ **Lyndon Pindling was one of the first leaders of the PLP. He later became the first premier and then prime minister of The Bahamas**

**Activity 2** Discuss the impact of historical events

Read the extract below. Discuss the questions that follow:

Until the 1950s, there were no political parties in The Bahamas. Only elected individuals could join the House of Assembly. A group of white businessmen held most of the power in the Assembly. They were known as the 'Bay Street Boys' because they were merchants who owned many businesses on Bay Street in Nassau.

1 Discuss how this situation changed in the 1950s.
2 Which parties were formed? Why? By whom?
3 What was the aim of each party?
4 Why do you think the PLP gained the support of ordinary citizens when it was formed? Give two reasons.

## The General Strike

In January 1958, the new international airport at Nassau was scheduled to open. The new airport would bring many tourists to The Bahamas. However, the government chose a foreign bus company to provide all the transport services from the airport to hotels. This angered Bahamian taxi drivers, who knew that the chosen company was linked to the 'Bay Street Boys', the same white businessmen that controlled the House of Assembly, and it led to what is known as the General Strike.

As a result of the strike, The Secretary of State for the colonies came to Nassau in June 1958 and ordered the first constitutional steps toward majority rule.

**Word power**

General Strike

▲ **After the general strike, Bahamians continued calling for equality on Labour Days in the 1950s and 1960s**

Read the extracts from different sources below before you do Activity 3.

On the morning of 2 November 1957, when the new airport opened for traffic, the Taxi Cab Union, led by Clifford Darling, blockaded all roads from the airport. The demonstration was supported by the PLP and The Bahamas Federation of Labour (BFL). Negotiations between the parties failed, and on Sunday, 12 January 1958, the general strike began. Hotels closed, racial tensions ran high, and troops were called in. By 21 January 1958, the tourist trade had come to a standstill, negatively affecting the local economy.



**From the Hansard, the official record of UK parliamentary discussion, dated 30 January 1958:**

**Mr Lennox Boyd:** The strike in The Bahamas originated from a dispute between two conflicting commercial interests and not from one between employers and employees. Stoppages of work by employees in public and private services, including the hotels, have since taken place. There has been no violence or disorder but as a precaution a company of troops has been flown in from Jamaica. This has provided much needed relief for the local police. H.M.S. "Ulster" went to Nassau for the purpose of providing technicians to maintain essential services. Utilities such as electricity and water have continued uninterrupted. Meetings have been taking place between representatives of the parties involved under impartial chairmanship. The Governor has been making continuous efforts to get the parties concerned to effect a settlement and, although I have no details as yet, I am glad to say that the strike is ending today.

**Tips**

Are there any words or phrases you don't understand? Try to work out what they mean in context. Use your dictionary to help you find the meanings if you cannot work them out.

**Did you know?**

Most parliaments have a Hansard. This is the written record of proceedings and debates in Parliament. It is a verified and accurate record of what is said in a session.

Work with a partner.

Read the information and newspaper headlines about the General Strike. Answer these questions about the strike:

1 What was the cause of this event?
2 How was it resolved?
3 Why was it an important event in the movement towards majority rule?

### The Woman's Suffrage Movement

In 1959, women in The Bahamas started the **Women's Suffrage Movement**. Mary Ingraham was the first president and Georgianna Symonette was the vice-president. They were joined by other powerful women, including Ruby Ann Cooper-Darling, Marguerite Pindling and Janet Bostwick.

The suffragettes petitioned for women's rights and they took up the matter of votes for women, arguing that the right to vote was universal and every adult should have that right (universal suffrage). Their efforts were successful – in July 1961, the vote for females became law. Ruby Ann Cooper-Darling was the first woman to register to vote. Women voted for the first time, in 1962, along with all men who had reached the age of 21.

**Word power**

Women's Suffrage Movement

◄ Bahamian suffragettes



1 Work with a partner. Watch the news article about Ruby Ann Cooper-Darling and her contributions to building our nation. You can find this on https://ournews.bs/scholarship-highlights-suffrage-movement-icon/

 a What did you learn about Reverend Cooper-Darling in this video?
 b What has been done to honour her life and work?

2 Why was universal suffrage important in our path to majority rule? Give two reasons.

## Black Tuesday

Lynden Pindling and other members of the opposition felt that the government was not addressing the concerns and needs of the Bahamian people adequately and that they were obstructing steps towards majority rule.

On 27 April 1965, in an act of protest and frustration, Lynden Pindling picked up the ceremonial mace, which symbolised the authority of the House, and threw it out of the window to a crowd of people who were gathered in Bay Street. Milo Butler then threw out the hourglass. These actions were a symbolic gesture expressing the frustration and desire for change among the opposition members. The day became known as **Black Tuesday**.

In August 1965, the PLP sent a delegation to address the United Nations Committee on Colonisation. They highlighted the problems of the majority of Bahamians and put the blame for many of those problems on the UBP's unwillingness to address them.

On 10 January 1967, majority rule was established in The Bahamas. The PLP won the most votes, but the PLP and the UBP each got 18 seats in the House of Assembly. Randol Fawkes (remember, he had one seat in parliament) and Alvin Braynen (who was elected as an Independent Candidate) both gave their support to the PLP to give them the majority of seats.

Sir Lynden Pindling became the first black Premier of The Bahamas. Alvin Braynen became the Speaker of the house.

▲ **This postage stamp shows the ceremonial mace used in parliament**

**Word power**

Black Tuesday

**Activity 5** Sequence the events leading to majority rule

Work in a group.

Prepare a large timeline for the period 1940 to 1975:

- Use your timeline to show key dates and important events on the road to majority rule.
- Include symbols and pictures.
- Add the names of political heroes who played important roles in each event.

**Activity 6** Why do we celebrate Majority Rule Day?

A group of visiting students asks you why your country has a national holiday called Majority Rule Day. What would you tell them?

## From majority rule to independence 1967–1973

Under majority rule, The Bahamas was still a British Colony, but the foundations of self-governance and independence had already been laid in our Constitution.

In 1969, in agreement with the British Colonial Government, the Constitution was amended to allow for the country to move towards full self-governance and independence. As a result of the amendments, the title of Premier was changed to Prime Minister.

Prime Minister Lynden Pindling set a target of 1973 for independence. Not everyone agreed – some PLP members left the party to join the newly formed Free National Movement (FNM).

In the 1972 elections, the PLP won a large majority of the seats in the House of Assembly. This allowed them to move forward with the process of becoming independent.

On 10 July 1973, The Bahamas officially gained independence from the United Kingdom and became an independent nation with its own Constitution, government, currency and national symbols. The name Colony of the Bahama Islands was changed to The Commonwealth of The Bahamas. Sir Lynden Pindling became the first Prime Minister and Sir Milo Butler became the first Governor-General of our independent nation.

## Activity 7 Add events to your timeline

Use the timeline you made in Activity 6. Add the key events from majority rule to independence. Again, include symbols and the names and roles of political heroes involved in the different events.

## Activity 8 What changed at independence?

Work with a partner to make a large 'Before and after' display to show important changes in our country after independence in 1973. Consider changes made to the following:

- the name of the country
- the structure of the government
- the flag
- our Coat of Arms
- the national anthem
- our currency
- membership of regional and international organisations
- our relationship with the UK.

## Activity 9 Write a speech for Independence Day celebrations

Work in pairs.

1 Discuss these questions:
   a When do we celebrate Independence Day?
   b How is this event celebrated in your community?
2 Imagine you have been asked to give a talk to younger students about Independence Day and its importance in our history.
   a What information would you include?
   b How would you make your speech interesting and engaging?
3 a Write a draft of your speech. Practise saying it out loud.
   b Once you are confident, try presenting your speech to another pair or to the class.

> **Tips**
>
> Keep the structure of your speech simple and clear. It should have an introduction, a body of speech, and a conclusion.

> **Reflection**
>
> You have been asked to suggest another national holiday. Work in groups to decide on a holiday. Tell the class the name of your holiday and why it should be celebrated.

# 16 Nation builders



## Building our nation

**Word power**

national hero
nation builder

Many of our Bahamian **national heroes** are people who empowered people to stand up for their rights and who worked hard to help our country achieve majority rule. These are the people we call **nation builders** – their bravery, commitment and hard work laid the foundation for the free, independent country we live in today.

In The Bahamas, we are very proud of our national heroes in different fields and we honour them in different ways. These are some of the ways in which nation builders are honoured:

**National honours**, such as the 'Order of The Bahamas' that recognise achievements in areas such as arts and culture, sports, science and innovation, education, public service and philanthropy.

▶ Her excellency, Dame Ivy Dumont at a national honours ceremony

**Statues and monuments** honour our national heroes, for example:

- The Sir Milo Butler Statue in Rawson Square in downtown Nassau honours our first Governor-General.
- The Sir Lynden Pindling Statue in Lynden Pindling Square pays tribute to our first Prime Minister.
- The Pompey Memorial in Steventon on Exuma is dedicated to the memory of Pompey, an enslaved African who led a rebellion against slavery.
- The Sir Roland Symonette statue in Alice Town, Bimini honours our first Premier.

▲ **The Pompey memorial in Steventon, Exuma reminds us of our heroes and our heritage**

**National museums and exhibitions**, such as the Pompey Museum of Slavery and Emancipation and the National Art Gallery of The Bahamas, showcase the achievements and contributions of nation builders. They can help to educate and inspire citizens.

These institutions keep and display artefacts, documents and stories related to these individuals so that visitors can learn about their impact on the nation's development.

**Creating educational scholarships and grants** in the name of nation builders can provide opportunities for aspiring individuals to pursue their passions and contribute to the nation's progress.

These financial aids are awarded to outstanding students or professionals in fields linked to the values and goals of the nation builders they are named for.

## Activity 1 Find evidence in your community

Work in pairs.

1 Make a list of street names, names of buildings and other institutions (schools, halls, libraries, bridges and so on) in your community that are named after national heroes.
2 Choose three names and discuss their contributions to our country.

# Political heroes

In the years before majority rule and independence, many people played important roles in building our nation. Two important people from that time are Sir Lynden Pindling and Randol Fawkes.

A Grade 6 class discussed the gifts and talents of different political heroes and how each person used their gifts and talents to help build our nation. They then wrote essays about each person. Below are the essays that two students wrote.

## Sir Lynden Pindling

Our first Prime Minister, Sir Lynden Pindling, possessed many gifts and talents that greatly contributed to nation building. One of his remarkable talents was his exceptional leadership skills. He had the ability to bring people together and inspire them to work towards a common goal.

Sir Lynden also possessed strong speaking skills, which meant he could captivate audiences with his words. He used his gift of speech to rally the people of The Bahamas, encouraging them to stand up for their rights and fight against injustice.

▲ **Lynden Pindling**

Sir Lynden also had a very good understanding of politics and he was a very clever thinker. He used these talents to negotiate with other countries and argue for The Bahamas on the international stage.

Through his leadership, speeches, and political skills, Sir Lynden Pindling played a huge role in shaping The Bahamas into the nation it is today.

## Sir Randol Fawkes

Sir Randol Fawkes had several gifts and talents that contributed to nation building. One of his exceptional talents was his strong commitment to social justice and workers' rights.

Fawkes fought tirelessly for fair treatment and better conditions for workers. His gift of empathy and understanding allowed him to connect with the struggles of working people and to voice their concerns.

▲ **Randol Fawkes**

Fawkes also had outstanding organising skills. He was able to get workers to act and he united them to fight for improved labour laws and equal rights. His dedication to justice and his organising skills helped create positive changes for workers in The Bahamas. Fawkes had excellent knowledge of the law, which he used to challenge unjust practices and promote equality.

Through his commitment to social justice, his organising skills and his legal knowledge, Randol Fawkes played a crucial role in nation building in The Bahamas by championing the rights and wellbeing of workers.

## Activity 2 Discussing political heroes

Read each essay carefully.

1 Identify the gifts and talents that made each person successful in their field.
2 Identify a gift or talent that you have. Write a few sentences explaining how you could use that gift or talent to contribute to your community and country.
3 Do your own research to find two ways that each of these nation builders have been honoured.

## Activity 3 Write your own essay

1 Choose another person who contributed politically to building our nation. The pictures on this page show some people you could consider.
2 Do your own research to find out about the person's gifts and talents and how he or she used these to contribute to nation building.
3 Then write your own essay about the person you chose.

▲ Mary Ingraham

▲ Clifford Darling

▲ Georgianna Symonette

▲ Dame Doris Johnson

▲ Clarence A. Bain

▲ Sir Stafford Sands

▲ Alvin Braynen

▲ Rome Italia Johnson

▲ Sir Cecil Wallace Whitfield

# Cultural and sporting heroes

People who achieve excellence in the fields of arts, culture and sport are also national heroes. We look up to them as role models. They often represent our country to the rest of the world.

## Sporting heroes

The Bahamas has some very well-known and popular sporting legends.

▲ The Golden Girls female relay team won gold at the 1999 Olympic Games

▲ The Golden Knights male relay team won gold in the 2012 Olympic Games

◄ Mark Knowles was the first Bahamian tennis player to reach No 1 status on the international tennis circuit. He is retired now, but he still works to develop tennis in our country

Today, Bahamian sportspeople continue to excel on the world stage in several sports, like the examples in the photos on the next page.

▲ Shaunae Miller-Uibo won gold medals for the 400 m at both the 2016 and 2020 Olympic Games

▲ Steven Gardiner won gold for the 400 m at the 2020 Olympic Games

## Activity 4 Watch our team win Olympic Gold

1 Find and watch video clips of the finals of the 1999 female relay and the 2012 male relay at the Olympic Games.

2 How do you think these events contributed to national pride? Think about how you felt watching these races and how Bahamians all around the world felt when each event happened.

3 Suggest two ways in which sportspeople like these contribute to nation building.

## Activity 5 Top 10 of the decade

In May 2023, the online magazine www.10thyearseniors.com published a list of the Top 10 Bahamian athletes of the decade 2010–2020. Here are the athletes on the list and the sport they excel at:

Tureano Johnson – Boxing

Byron Ferguson – Basketball

Jazz Chisholm – Baseball

Ariana Vanderpool-Wallace – Swimming

Antoan Richardson – Baseball

Deandre Ayton – Basketball

Jonquel Jones – Basketball

Steven Gardiner – Athletics

Buddy Hield – Basketball

Shaunae Miller-Uibo – Athletics

Work in a group.

Imagine you have been asked to pick the Top 10 rising star athletes for the decade 2020–2030.

1 Who would you pick? Make a list of their names, where they come from and what sport they play.

2 Share your list with the class, giving reasons for your choices.

## Art and music

Who are the cultural leaders in the fields of art and music that inspire you? Read about some nation builders in these fields.

▲ **Stanley Burnside**

Stanley Burnside is a world-renowned painter and pioneer of a style of art called Afrofuturism.

Burnside uses natural elements and mystical symbolism from his heritage in his work which focuses on experiences of Africans in the Caribbean. In 2022, he exhibited his work in Nassau and had a large exhibition in New York.

▲ **Stanley Burnside's painting of Judas**

### Activity 6 Find out more about local artists

1 Work in a group.

  **a** Discuss Stanley Burnside's painting. How would you describe his style?

  **b** Do an internet search to find more of his artworks. Discuss how they make you feel and what you like about them.

2 Choose two of these Bahamian artists and find out about their life and work. Write a short biography of each person. Include pictures of their work, if you can.

- Gabrielle Banks
- Tamika Galanis
- Anina Major
- Averia Wright
- Jodi Mannis
- Brent Malone
- Antonius Roberts
- Maxwell Taylor
- Eddie Minnis

3 Find out about other Bahamian artists from your island or community. Make a class display to highlight their work.

Music and dance have always been important in our culture. This is celebrated during Junkanoo and other music and dance festivals.

Goombay music is one of the earliest types of indigenous music. It can be traced back to the drumbeat rhythms of Africa. This style of music was used by many early Bahamian musicians and composers like Blind Blake, George Symonette and Eloise Lewis.

Rake 'n' Scrape, which comes from the Cat Islands, is a popular form of folk music that is used by many composers and musicians. Eddie Minnis and Ronnie Butler are well-known Rake 'n' Scrape artists.

## Activity 7 Compile a playlist

Imagine you have been asked to make a playlist to highlight Bahamian musicians who are nation builders.

Which artists would you include? Why?

What would be the top 3 songs on your playlist? Why?

## Religious leaders

There are many examples of religious leaders who are national heroes. Read about two of them.

### Reverend Angela Palacious

The first female deacon and Anglican priest in The Bahamas. She is also an author of eight books.

▲ **Reverend Angela Palacious**

### Father Jerome

An architect who became an Anglican missionary. He built four churches on Cat Island, as well as a medical clinic, convent/monastery (the hermitage), technical school, and other projects throughout The Bahamas.

▲ **Father Jerome**

## Activity 8 Research leaders in your community

Work with a partner.

1 Choose one religious or community leader that you regard as a nation builder. Write a short research paper about their life.

2 a Try to identify the moment or achievement that made them a nation builder.

 b Describe the impact of their work for past and future generations.

### Reflection

Identify a leader who has had a positive effect on your daily life. Explain what the person did to have this effect.

# 17 Traditions and culture



## What is culture?

**Word power**

culture

The food you eat, the clothes you wear, the music you listen to, the books you read, how you worship, what you believe and the ways in which you behave are all part of your **culture**. Sharing the same experiences and behaving in similar ways to other people can make us feel like we are part of a group because we share the same culture.

The pictures show some things that people may describe as part of their culture.

▲ Music

▲ Art

▲ Traditional food

▲ Festivals

▲ Crafts

▲ Sailing

**Activity 1** Make a collage

Work in groups. Think about Bahamian culture.

1  Brainstorm a list of cultural behaviours that are shared by many Bahamians. For example, many people like to share a plate and enjoy food with friends and family; many people believe it is important to honour and show respect for their elders.

2  Make a collage to show at least ten different aspects of Bahamian culture today.

3  Think about where these cultural behaviours come from. Share your ideas with your group.

**Activity 2** Language and culture

If you hear someone speak, you can often tell that they are Bahamian by listening to their accent. Bahamians also use many words and phrases that other Bahamians recognise and understand. For example, most people know that a *potcake* is a mixed-breed dog, and that the answer to *'What da wybe is?'* sometimes is *'een nothin'*.

1  Work in groups. Make a list of some expressions that you and your friends use. Which of these expressions come from Bahamian culture?

2  Which expressions come from other cultures? How do you think they have become part of youth culture?

# History and culture

Bahamian culture today has strong links with the culture of our ancestors from different places including Africa, Britain and the Americas.

Our unique Bahamian culture and way of life has developed and changed over many generations. Our way of life today is very different from that of our ancestors, but their influence can be seen in:

- buildings and ruins
- our language and expressions
- the foods we eat and how we prepare them
- music and musical instruments
- literature (including folk tales) and art
- religion and beliefs
- feasts and festivals.

▲ Antonius Roberts carved these wooden African figures. The display is called 'Sacred Space' and it is a tribute to our African ancestry. The figures mostly face east, in the direction of Africa. The display is located near where ships unloaded some of the first enslaved people

## Activity 3 Buildings and ruins

1 Vendue House is a historic building in Nassau. In the past slave auctions were held there. Today it is home to the Pompey Museum of Slavery and Emancipation. What can we learn about our ancestors and culture from museums?

2 Find out about these buildings and ruins. Write two sentences about what each one tells you about Bahamian history and culture.

- Deveaux Plantation (Cat Island)
- French Cloisters (Paradise Island)
- Fort Charlotte (Nassau)
- Original Wesley Methodist Church (Eleuthera)

▲ **Vendue House in Nassau**

## Activity 4 Historical events and their influence on culture

1 Work in groups. Discuss what you know about each of these important events in our history:

- Lucayans settle in The Bahamas
- The arrival of Christopher Columbus
- The golden age of piracy
- Colonisation by the British
- Trans-Atlantic trade in enslaved people
- Majority rule
- The development of tourism
- Independence

2 Choose two of the historical events. Write short notes about how each event influenced Bahamian culture. Think about language, dance and music, art, food, clothing, festivals and celebrations and worship.

### Reflection

Think about any person who lived in The Bahamas in the 1800s. What would be the same for them if they could visit the islands today? What would be very different?

## Activity 5 Mini-project – culture and change

It is easy to see how modern culture and our way of life today is different from that of the Lucayans, enslaved Africans, and early British settlers. Now you are going to find out how our culture and way of life have changed in more recent times.

You are going to interview an adult in your community. The person you interview must be at least 20 years older than you.

1 Prepare a short questionnaire for the interview. Here are some ideas that you can use to write your questions.

- How have traditional fishing or farming changed since you were a child?

- What are some differences in the ways people dress today compared to when you were a child?

- Have there been any changes in the types of food that are commonly eaten in our community? Are there any new dishes or ingredients that have become popular?

- Have conservation efforts affected the way people interact with and care for the natural resources around our island?

- How has transport, like boats or planes, improved or changed over the past 20 years? Have these changes affected how people travel to and from our island?

- Have traditional celebrations or festivals, such as Junkanoo, changed in any ways? If so, how?

- How has the use of technology, like smartphones and the internet, changed the way people in our community live their daily lives?

- Do you think the ways that people socialise and interact with each other in our community has changed over the past 20 years? For example, do social media or online platforms affect how people connect and communicate?

2 Share what you find out with your group.

3 Write a short essay describing how the culture and way of life in your community has changed in recent times. Include examples and quotes from your interview.

### Connections

# Different countries, different cultures

This diagram show some of the ways in which we can learn about other cultures:

**Reading** – books, stories, folktales and information books.

**Media** – watching films, documentaries and even the news.

**Music** – rhythms and lyrics from different countries.

**Languages** – hearing how people greet and talk to each other.

**Online resources** – websites, apps and videos allow you to explore culture, art, heritage and music. You can even ask an AI to tell you about different cultures.

**Travel** – real trips or virtual tours allow us to interact with people and learn about their way of life.

**Festivals and celebrations** – attending or learning about celebrations tells you about music, dance, food and other traditions.

**Museums and galleries** – displays and information about culture and history. Many museums and galleries now offer virtual tours online.

We can also learn about culture from people themselves. When people visit our country, we learn about them and their way of life. When we travel and visit other places, we meet people and learn about their culture and way of life.

When we try to learn about other cultures, we must be careful not to generalise. When we **generalise**, we say something as if it applies to everyone, even if some people don't fit what we are saying. Another word for generalisation is **stereotype**. Stereotypes are usually unfair and untrue generalisations. Below are some examples. Can you think of any others?

All Bahamians live on the beach.

All Scottish people wear kilts.

All Americans are rich.

**Word power**

generalise
stereotype

Activity 6 Read about other cultures

An online magazine asked three children from different countries to write a short blog post about their culture and way of life.

1 Read each blog post that follows with a partner.

2 Discuss what you can learn about each culture from these blog posts.

**Connections**

# Jannali – Australia

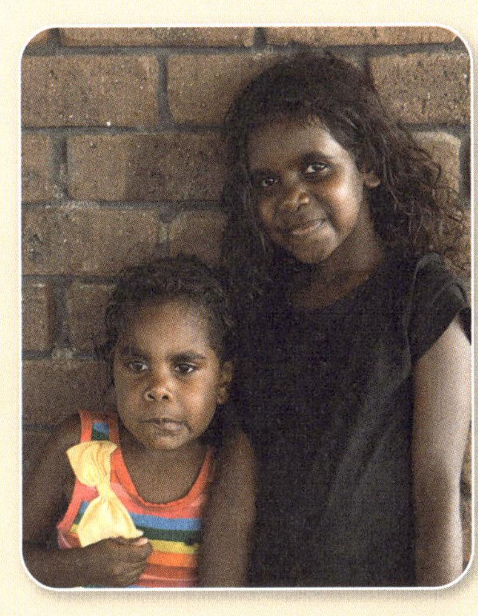

G'day! I'm Jannali. I live in Coffs Harbour in Australia. My mom's family are Italian, and my dad is Gumbaynggirr. I'm happy to tell you about our culture and way of life.

Let's start with food. My mom makes the most delicious pasta and pizzas, and I can't get enough of her homemade gelato (ice-cream). When we visit Dad's mob (that's what he calls his family), we get to taste incredible bush foods. We often go fishing, and then my uncles cook over a fire outside. I love learning about different ingredients and cooking techniques from both sides of my family.

One of the best things about my dad's family is their deep connection to the land. My dad calls where he comes from his country. When we go to visit his country, it is so different from being in town. I feel a special bond when we go there, surrounded by nature and the stories that have been passed down for generations. My aunties and uncles teach me about the Dreamtime and the importance of taking care of the land and everything in it.

My nan takes me on nature walks and she told me that Gumbaynggirr were always known as the 'sharing people'. They got this name because their land was so rich that they often shared food and other resources with other nations. My nan is a great artist and she often has exhibitions of her paintings.

My family try hard to respect and learn from different cultures. I'm proud to honour my Italian roots and the Gumbaynggirr heritage. It is like having the best of both worlds, and I wouldn't trade it for anything.

# Luca – Switzerland

Grüessech, I'm Luca, a Swiss boy from Wengen village. My family is traditional, and we love our little village and the beautiful nature that surrounds us.

Living in a small village has ups and downs. Everyone knows each other, and there is a strong sense of community. Each year we take part in some traditional events like the cow parades, where cows come down from the mountains, decorated with beautiful flowers and bells. We also have folklore festivals where we wear traditional Swiss costumes and dance to lively music.

Food is important in our family. I love fondue and raclette. It is so much fun gathering around the table, melting cheese and dipping in bread or potatoes with family and friends. And of course, I think Switzerland has the best chocolate in the world!

Nature is a big part of our way of life. We are surrounded by stunning mountains, and me and my friends love hiking, skiing, and exploring the outdoors. I'm learning to snowboard.

My parents value tradition and hard work. They try to teach me to appreciate the simple things in life and they believe in taking care of one another. My dad says it important to preserve traditions and to make sure they don't die out.

# Pedro – Brazil

Oi! I'm Pedro, from São Paulo in Brazil. Growing up in Brazil is like having a big, noisy, colourful party every day. Let me tell you about my family and our way of life!

Family is everything to Brazilians. I have a big, extended family with uncles, aunts, cousins, and grandparents who are always around. Our family gatherings are lively and filled with delicious food. My favourite is the feijoada, a black bean stew with lots of meat! It is a traditional dish we enjoy on special occasions.

After family, I would put soccer. Brazilians generally love soccer! It is like a religion here, and playing soccer with my friends is pure joy.

And after soccer, we like to dance and party. From the rhythms of samba and bossa nova to the energetic capoeira, our music and dance scenes are amazing. I love playing the pandeiro and shaking my body to the beats of Brazilian music.

We also have famous celebrations like Carnaval, where the whole country comes alive with colourful costumes, parades, and samba parties!

Brazil has a mix of indigenous, African, and European influences that make us unique. I am proud of our history and the rich culture that has come from it. In our country we celebrate our heritage through food,

music, dance, and festivals that bring people together from all walks of life.

**Activity 7** Compare the blogs

1 Copy this table into your notebook. Write two statements in each box to compare these children's culture and way of life with yours.

|  | How our culture and way of life are the same | How our culture and way of life are different |
| --- | --- | --- |
| Jannali |  |  |
| Luca |  |  |
| Pedro |  |  |

2 Discuss with your group which child's culture and way of life is most like yours and suggest three reasons for this.

Keshia and Rayshawn wanted to know more about the culture of South Africa and Japan. They did some research and made these short notes.

## Japan

- Island nation – archipelago in the Pacific Ocean
- Frequent natural disasters – preparedness/community cooperation
- Ancient Japan – Shinto religion, system of aristocracy, focus on poetry and tea ceremonies, samurai warriors and honour-based systems, spread of Zen Buddhism, traditional arts and Noh theatre, and developments in tea ceremony
- 1600–1868 – period of isolation from rest of the world, Kabuki theatre and changes to the tea ceremony
- 1868 onwards – period of restoration, modernisation and westernisation, modern education system
- World War II had a devastating effect; atomic bombs dropped on Nagasaki and Hiroshima
- After the war – economic miracle, technological advancement, culture of hard work and innovation
- Modern pop culture – anime, manga comics, fashion and entertainment
- Cherry Blossom Festival in spring each year

### South Africa

- Before 1650 – indigenous people, San, Khoikhoi and various Bantu-speaking groups; language, art and strong oral traditions
- European colonisation – Dutch and then British, European languages, Christianity and forced labour (slavery); enslaved people from Malaysia and other Dutch colonies in East Indies brought to the Cape; Indians brought as forced labourers for sugar plantations on east coast
- Conflict between Dutch descendants ('Boers') and British colonisers
- Discovery of gold and diamonds; rapid influx of people and growth of towns and cities; migrant labour system
- From 1948 – government imposed racial segregation (apartheid) and limited rights for black people; uprisings and protest lead to violence and international sanctions.
- Nelson Mandela is released from prison and becomes first democratically elected president in 1994. The country moves away from apartheid towards human rights and democracy; modern Constitution , 11 national languages
- Festivals and celebrations: New Year, Cape Malay Carnival, Heritage Day
- Diverse music, dance and food

## Activity 8 Research other cultures

Work in groups.

1 Discuss the short notes about each country. What can each point tell you about the culture and way of life in that country?

2 Where could you find up-to-date reliable information about each country to learn more about its culture and how people live? Choose the three best suggestions and use them to find out more about each country.

3 Prepare a short oral or audio-visual presentation for the class to teach them more about the culture and way of life of people in South Africa and Japan today.

**Reflection**

Which elements of each country's culture were familiar to you? Which were unfamiliar?

## Theme 3 What have you learnt?

### Unit 14 Learning about the past

**1** Who were the indigenous inhabitants of The Bahamas when Christopher Columbus made landfall?

**2** How did the arrival of European settlers affect the indigenous inhabitants?

**3** Complete this table about three groups of people who chose to settle in The Bahamas.

|  | Eleutheran Adventurers | Pirates | Loyalists |
|---|---|---|---|
| Who were they? |  |  |  |
| Why did they come to The Bahamas? |  |  |  |
| When did they come here? |  |  |  |
| Where did they settle? |  |  |  |
| How did their actions affect our society? |  |  |  |
| What evidence can we find of their influence today? |  |  |  |

**4** Write a short essay explaining how enslaved Africans brought to The Bahamas contributed to building our nation. Include information about how and why we celebrate Emancipation Day on the first Monday of August each year.

### Unit 15 Bahamian history prior to independence

**5** Define the following terms:

   **a** The Contract

   **b** majority rule

   **c** colonial government

   **d** independence

   **e** universal suffrage.

**6** For each year, state one important event that happened and why it was important in our history.

( 1942 ) ( 1953 ) ( 1958 ) ( 1962 ) ( 1965 ) ( 1967 )

## (Continued)

**7** Complete this table to compare the government in our country at various stages in our history.

| | Before majority rule | After majority rule | After independence |
|---|---|---|---|
| Leadership (titles and persons) | | | |
| Form of government | | | |
| Who was allowed to vote? | | | |

**8** Why is Sir Lynden Pindling called the father of our nation? Give two reasons.

**9** When did The Commonwealth of The Bahamas come into existence?

## Unit 16 Nation builders

**10** Sir Milo Butler is considered to be a political hero.

   **a** Give two reasons why Sir Milo Butler is a political hero.

   **b** Name two women who can be considered to be political heroes. Give a reason for each choice.

   **c** What role did Sir Randol Fawkes play in building our nation?

**11** Who is your favourite sporting hero? Explain what makes this person a good role model and how they contribute to nation building.

**12** How do artists like Stanley Burnside contribute to our sense of national pride and help to build our nation?

**13** Can musicians be nation builders? Support your answer.

## Unit 17 Traditions and culture

**14** Explain why Junkanoo is important in our culture.

**15** What makes a person Bahamian? Draw and label pictures to answer this question.

**16** In South Africa, the discovery of gold and diamonds meant that many men left their homes and families and travelled to mining areas to work on contracts.

   **a** How do you think this affected their communities and the families they left behind?

   **b** What event in our history is similar to this?

**17** Choose one of the countries that you studied (Australia, Brazil, Japan, South Africa or Switzerland). Write a paragraph describing what you learnt about the culture and heritage of that country.

# Glossary

## A

**Act of Parliament:** a law written and passed by parliament, which must then be followed by the whole country

**agency; agencies:** (of the United Nations) smaller groups within the UN that deal with specific issues

**ambassador:** head of a country's embassy, representing their own country in a foreign country; citizens of a country that take pride in promoting their country and culture

## B

**ballot:** a specially printed form on which people cast their votes at a polling station

**bank:** a financial institution that uses money from their investors to let the government or other people borrow money (capital) for expensive projects

**bill:** a draft proposal for a new law that parliament will debate, change and vote on whether to pass or not

**Black Tuesday:** day on which Lynden Pindling and Milo Butler protested in parliament with a symbolic gesture expressing the desire for change towards majority rule, by throwing the ceremonial mace and hourglass out of a window

**budget:** a financial plan for estimating how much money will be earned and spent

**Burma Road riot:** a protest in 1942 about unfair labour practices related to how Bahamian workers were paid unfair wages for the construction of US air bases in The Bahamas.

## C

**cabinet:** the Prime Minister and the ministers that are responsible for running the government

**campaign:** different methods, such as posters, home visits or mass rallies, that political parties use to try and convince people to vote for them

**citizen:** a person who is recognised by law as a member of a country

**civil servant:** a person who works in the public sector, employed by the government, government agencies or government-owned businesses

**climate change:** how the temperature and rainfall patterns of a region change over time

**coastline:** the boundary where a sea, gulf or ocean meets the land

**communication:** sharing information, news and ideas

**constable:** a local police officer that helps with law enforcement

**Constitution:** the highest laws of a country

**continent:** one of the seven large bodies of land on Earth, separated by oceans

**Contract, The:** an agreement made in the 1940s between The Bahamas and the USA that granted Bahamian workers seasonal contracts to work in the USA

**coordinates:** the specific location of any place on Earth, written as the line of latitude closest to it, followed by the line of longitude

**country:** an independent nation with its own government

**culture:** everything we do that shows we are part of a community with its own traditions

## D

**debate:** discussing a bill in parliament in detail, taking the views of different parties into account before MPs vote on whether to pass it or not

**defendant:** a person accused of a crime and whose case is being heard in court

**democracy:** a country where citizens of the state elect the leaders they want to represent them

**dictatorship:** a country ruled by one person or a small group of people with absolute power and usually without an election or Constitution

**dissolving:** breaking up, ending – such as the dissolving of a government before an election is held

## E

**economy:** the goods and services produced in the country

**election day:** a day on which citizens of a democratic country vote to choose representatives for a new government

**election:** the process in a democratic country where adult citizens vote to choose the people or political parties they want to represent them

**era:** a period of time in history

**executive:** the head of state and the ministries that run the country

## F

**finances:** matters related to the money needed to run the country or one's own financial matters

## G

**General Strike:** a large-scale strike in 1958 because of unfair labour practices by the government during the construction of a new international airport in Nassau

**generalise:** saying something as if it applies to everyone, even when it only applies to some individuals

**global warming:** the rise in the average temperature of the Earth from excessive carbon dioxide caused by the burning of fossil fuels

**government:** organisation that runs a state and keeps law and order in an independent state

**greenhouse gases:** carbon dioxide and other gases that trap heat in the atmosphere

**gulf:** part of a sea that extends far into the land

## H

**hemisphere:** half of the Earth, as divided by imaginary lines – 0° line of longitude (Prime Meridian) divides the Earth into the eastern and western hemispheres; 0° line of latitude (Equator) divides the Earth into the northern and southern hemispheres

**history:** the study of events and people from the past

**human resources:** people who use their ideas and work to provide services or make goods

## I

**island:** land area that is smaller than a continent and surrounded by water

## J

**judiciary:** the judges and courts that make sure the laws are obeyed and that the government itself upholds the Constitution of the country

**jury:** ordinary men and women who are asked to listen to the evidence presented in a Supreme Court case before they vote on whether a defendant is guilty or not

**Justice of the Peace:** a local official with the same powers as a magistrate to sign and to issue warrants

## L

**landlocked:** countries that are surrounded by other countries and do not have a coastline

**latitude:** imaginary lines that run from east to west on maps of the Earth

**legislature:** the group of people who make laws

**longitude:** imaginary lines that run from north to south on maps of the Earth; also called meridians

## M

**magistrate:** the official presiding over a Magistrate's Court, hearing evidence and deciding whether a defendant is guilty or not

**majority rule:** a political system where the party that gets the most votes in a general election gets to govern the country, with all citizens accepting their right to govern

**manufacturing:** making goods

**monarchy:** a country that has a monarch as the head of state

## N

**nation builder:** a person who shows/showed bravery, commitment and hard work in working towards the welfare of the country's citizens

**national hero:** a person who empowered others to stand up for their rights and who worked hard to help our country achieve majority rule

**national pride:** when you love your country and feel proud of its achievements and culture

**natural disaster:** natural events that can cause damage to property and the environment, and that harm people, such as earthquakes

**nomination:** notification of any independent person or political party that they intend to stand for an election

## O

**ocean:** one of the large bodies of salt water between and around the continents

## P

**physical map:** a map showing the natural features of an area

**political map:** a map showing human-made features of an area

**Project, The:** the construction of US air bases in The Bahamas which led to the Burma Road riot in protest against unfair labour practices

## R

**referendum:** a special voting process during which the government must get approval from its citizens for any proposed changes to the Constitution that will affect their rights or freedoms

**republic:** any state where the government is elected by the people and the president rules without a monarch

## S

**sea:** smaller part of an ocean that is close to land

**source:** information that helps us build up a picture of what happened in the past; can be written material, such as diaries and letters, or physical remains, such as buildings and other artefacts

**stereotype:** another word for generalisation

**symbol:** object or sign that represents a value or feeling, such as the symbols on our Coat of Arms

## T

**timeline:** a diagram for showing the order of events in the past, with dates and information about major events

**transportation:** moving goods, documents or people from place to place, using different means of transport

## U

**unconstitutional:** any action that is not in line with what is specified in the country's highest law, the Constitution

## W

**Women's Suffrage Movement:** the campaign by women, who became known as suffragettes, for women to get the right to vote in government elections